NEON DREAMS

The Story of the
Texas Pegasus
and the
Man Who Created It

Gwen Trammell McMath

Neon Dreams

© 2020 by Gwen Trammell McMath

All rights reserved. This book or any portion thereof may not be reproduced or used in any manner whatsoever without the express written permission of the publisher except for the use of brief quotations in a book review.

ISBN (Print): 978-1-09832-797-2
ISBN (eBook): 978-1-09832-798-9

For my Family: Vanessa and Charley (in heaven),
Neil, Amber, Charlie, Tom, Elizabeth, Robin,
Augie, Shep, and Jack, all my love forever.

Gwen gets to the heart of a Texas treasure in the person of J.B. McMath and his beloved "Flying Red Horse." Her book is not only a labor of love, but is utterly interesting and entertaining.

> LARRY MCCLENNY, Church of Christ minister, former superintendent of Patton Springs ISD, Afton, Texas

Gwen McMath reminds us of the value of family. The stories she shares gives us a vivid example of how one person can impact the lives of others one generation at a time. You will be blessed by this legacy of faith in God.

> DR. CONNIE COLE JESKE, Pastor of First United Methodist Church of Tulsa, Oklahoma, author of Who Is My Neighbor, available through Amazon Press.

It is easy to think of history as a recitation of facts and dates, but the best kind of history tells a story that puts you in the shoes of the people who lived it. Gwen McMath has crafted a story of history that deserves to be remembered, while also honoring the legacy of the family of her late husband – one of the most passionate Texas historians whom I had the privilege of knowing.

> MACHAIA V. MCCLENNY, History Researcher, The Alamo

"Neon Dreams" tells the story of both the iconic "Flying Red Horse" neon sign, perched atop the Magnolia Building in downtown Dallas, and the ambitions of a unique, yet quintessentially Texan family. Rendered with passion, grace, and a loving regard for her home state, "Neon Dreams" is a must read for anyone hoping to appreciate the soul of modern Texas.

> DR. DAVID BLANKE is the Paul and Frances Haas Professor of History at Texas A&M University-Corpus Christi, where he teaches and writes about U.S. Modern Popular Culture. He is the author of "Cecil B. DeMille, Classical Hollywood and Modern American Mass Culture: 1910-1960," published in 2018, "Hell on Wheels: The Promise and Peril of America's Car Culture, 1900-1940, published 2007, "Sowing the American Dream: How Consumer Culture Took Root in the Rural Midwest," published in 2000, and "The 1910s (American Popular Culture Through History," published in 2002, and "A Destiny of Choice?: New Directions in American Consumer History, published in 2013, all available through Amazon Press.

Preface

When I was a young girl living in Grand Prairie, Texas (a suburb of Dallas) everyone knew the icon of the "Flying Red Horse." It was a beautiful red neon flying horse (Pegasus) that was placed on the top of the then tallest building in downtown Dallas, the Mobil Oil Building. Each time I would go from my home in Grand Prairie toward Dallas at night my parents would say to me, "Look Gwen, it's the Flying Red Horse!" I always admired it and had no idea that several years later I would marry the grandson of the man who designed and built it, Charley McMath. I would come to know and believe that my marriage to Charley was providential in many ways.

Marrying into the McMath family in 1968, I immediately began to notice the different traditions of our families. One of the biggest differences was the attitude about family history. My husband, Charley, was interested in all things historical so he wanted to keep all historical records, etc., from both sides of the family. In addition to this, his grandparents J.B. and Mae McMath also kept everything historical about the family. Mae was kind of a "paper hoarder" in that if she received any slip of paper that had Bible scriptures on it she would save it because she felt it would be terrible to throw away something with the word of God on it. So when the grandparents died, Charley inherited all of their historical records. We continued to move around with this huge filing cabinet full of papers through all our meanderings across Texas over the next thirty years. I always thought that when Charley retired as a school administrator he would go through all of this history and write a book.

As providence would have it, things did not work out that way. Shortly before my husband retired he was diagnosed with lung cancer and he died ten months later. During the time after his death I still had all the family documents and they were in no order whatsoever. I felt sure that with my own death the wealth of material would all be thrown away, which was honestly very tempting for me to do at times. So I decided in a weak moment a few years ago to take on the task of sorting out all the documents and pictures and at least put them in chronological order. As I began to go through the material, I discovered that Charley's granddad had not only kept all the news documentation of his life but he had also written a very good biographical memoir of his life. J.B. was a wonderful man and one that I felt had greatness in two areas, business and spirituality. Not only had he described his life in the early 1900's but also accurately described everyday life in Dallas during that time as well.

It took me a few years to wade through all the material he had left behind and the more I read, the more I felt that his life should be shared with others. So here I am not being an original McMath but writing this story mainly because I was the one left with the material. Another note from granddaddy that convinced me to write down his memories was a quote from him I found one day while I was looking over his things. It said, "To relate the many wonderful things God has done for me, and the many things He has helped me to do, would require a book. While I fully realize such a book would be of little interest to any but relatives and close friends, I nevertheless hope some day to finish a book I have already started, as a gift to members of the family and friends."

The one thing I am an expert at is knowing how much of a wonderful man J.B. and his wife Mae were, they were mentors to me and taught me life lessons that I have never forgotten. I hope you enjoy their stories as much as I did researching and writing them. This story is both a historical and spiritual one, you will find as I did that there would be no way to separate the two.

Contents

Preface vii

Chapter 1   Perspectives of a Child: J.B.'s Childhood Memories 1

Chapter 2   God Comes Calling 12

Chapter 3   J.B.'s Brother Dale and his World War 1 Experiences Including his Dream or Night Vision by J.B. McMath, Sr. 39

Chapter 4   Dallas 1917 44

Chapter 5   The history of Neon Signs in the State of Texas 65

Chapter 6   Taking Time to Help Someone by J.B. McMath Sr. 87

Chapter 7   H.H. Wineburgh (previous owner of Texlite) The Story of Texlite taken from the periodical Texlite News, 15 May. 1951 91

Chapter 8   Relationship with J.J. "Jack Axilrod" Business Partner by J.B. McMath 109

Chapter 9   The History of the McAx Corporation as written by J.B. McMath, Sr. 117

Chapter 10 The Story of the Magnolia Building from the book The Unauthorized History of Dallas, Texas by Rose-Mary Rumbley, 1991. 124

Chapter 11 Periodical Documents and personal letter from the 1950's 128

Chapter 12 Beginnings of Christ for the Nations and a New Age of the Outpouring of the Holy Spirit in the 1960's 133

Chapter 13 Additional Newspaper Articles from the 1960's, Prayer and Another Dream 143

Chapter 14 Personal Healing of 1976 by J.B. McMath, Sr. and Articles from the 1970's 159

Chapter 15 The Eighties: The Final Chapter 164

Chapter 15 The Final Chapter 168

Chapter 16 Pegasus Finds a New Resting Place in Dallas 193

Author's Note 200

Dunlap, James, "Red steed still flying, Mr. Mac's story will knock you over." Dallas Morning News, 10 November 1975.

Frozen in flight, the Flying Red Horse atop the Mobil Building in Downtown Dallas seems to be locked in a perpetual struggle to soar over the structures of steel, concrete and glass that now tower over it.

The noble steed no longer turns. And Mobil turned off the clusters of lights that once spotted it at night two years ago at the onset of the energy crisis. The oil company says it probably won't ever be turned on again.

The horse can't be seen from a distance anymore, except at certain angles, and then it suddenly appears, stranded in a jungle of modern, taller office buildings.

But there was a time when the telephone switchboards at Mobil were jammed with concerned callers whenever the Flying Red Horse stopped turning. Atop its metal throne on what was once the tallest building in Dallas, the horse was the region's key landmark.

It was visible for miles; some pilots claimed they could see it from as far as Waco. The steel Pegasus was an object of awe and fascination for generations of children who grew up in the sign's heyday.

Nowadays, children have voyages to the moon and the outer reaches of the solar system to capture their imaginations, and the horse has even started to fade from the memories of the people who once revered it.

For at least one man living here, the mental image is just as clear as it ever was.

With ease, J.B. McMath can conjure up every contour. But then, he ought to, because he engineered the sign and supervised its installation in the fall of 1934.

"We called in two professional engineers and they said it was impractical and hazardous and they wouldn't have anything to do with it," McMath recalled as he sat in his small office at his home in East Dallas. Then he laughed and said, "And its still here 41 years later."

Surrounded by books, model train engines, files crammed with family history and photographs of his family and former employees and business associates, the 81-year-old, silver-haired man drifted back over the years to that fall.

In early September, 1934, an advertising man for Magnolia Oil Company, which merged with Mobil in 1959, contracted the Texlite sign company here and said Magnolia wanted a neon-lit Flying Red Horse revolving on top of its building at Main and Akard by Nov. 8 when the National Petroleum Institute would open its annual convention there.

Considering the size of the sign, the height of the building (29 stories or 350 feet), the wind factor and the amount of time for construction, it was a stiff order, but Texlite accepted it.

The task of engineering and installing the horse and making sure it was burning brightly come November was pitched into the lap of McMath, the company's treasurer and chief engineer.

Always up for a challenge, Mr. Mac, as he was known in those days, started making plans, ordered parts and went to California to get a mechanism to turn the sign and keep it anchored in the wind.

Once the materials were assembled, only six weeks remained before the convention's opening day and Texlite still had to keep up with its other orders from all over the country.

The Flying Red Horse, which actually consists of two horses joined in the middle by a system of metal struts McMath designed, is 30 by 40-feet, but each horse was constructed from smaller, separate pieces.

The smaller pieces were taken to the top floor in an elevator, passed out a window and hauled up to the roof for assembly, and gradually the sign took shape.

"Wait a minute," McMath said, interrupting his narrative, "I have a story that will knock you over."

Five days before Nov. 8 that horse was all up, except for the 1,162 feet of red neon tubing that would illuminate it. The tubing had been kept off until the last minute to prevent breakage, but this precaution almost ruined the whole project.

A fire swept through the Texlite plant, destroying all the tubing and, even more important, all the plans.

An important neon tube construction operation was quickly set up and McMath's crew got up on the horse high above the streets of downtown and made a pattern out of beaverboard.

Before the fire, McMath had only supervised, but after it happened and time was running out, everybody was up there working.

Dressed in his business clothes, McMath, then 40, drilled holes, bolted bolts and did anything that needed doing to get the job finished.

"If we hadn't finished it in time, we might have lost the Magnolia account," McMath said, explaining the necessity of meeting the contract deadline.

But the long hours of overtime and perseverance paid off because the sign was turned on the night of Nov. 7 and was ready to greet conventioneers the next day.

"I give God the honor for helping me by giving me the strength and the wisdom and the cooperation of the fine people I had working for me," McMath said.

Several nights after the sign was first turned on, after a call from one of Texlite's employees, McMath looked out the front door of his house and saw a whirling red blob. The Flying Red Horse had broken loose.

The horse was finally tied down, and McMath used a larger engine and a wind velocity thermostat to correct the problem. Since then, the Flying Red Horse has steadfastly maintained his post.

"It has stood a lot of storms," he said matter-of-factly. "Yeah, there's been a lot of wind service on that old sign."

When you consider that the sign weighs 6,000 pounds, its size and how long it has stayed up there, the Flying Red Horse represents a significant engineering feat for a man who never even graduated from high school.

"I always was mechanical," McMath explained. "I was just a practical engineer, born to be one."

He was born in Arkansas and lived in several Texas towns before he came to Dallas in 1917. Along the way, he gained the experience he would eventually draw upon to construct his masterpiece by working in a blacksmith shop, a sheet metal shop and as a sign painter's apprentice.

Although McMath admitted that his body is getting old, his mind is still clear and precise and his memory can retrieve dates, events and names like a computer.

"I always was a perfectionist," he said. "Never made a failure. Never had a customer turn down anything I made." McMath spoke the facts of his long career with pride, but it didn't come across as bragging. Just facts.

When McMath got in Dallas he became construction foreman for the Borich Sign Co., which was then one of the few electric sign companies in the country.

At that time, Borich was getting his signs from another company, but after five years of trying, McMath convinced his company that it could make better signs for less money.

Texlite was formed and opened on Trezevant Street in South Dallas in 1923 in a small building McMath built himself.

A year later, Texlite was bought out by another company, and with its added capital and New York City office, it grew into a national concern. McMath stayed on and became the company's treasurer and chief engineer.

In 1946, McMath and a man named Axilrod opened their own company, which eventually was called McAx Sign Co. In 1961, construction of R.L. Thornton Freeway claimed its Third Avenue plant, and McMath moved it to McGregor near Waco. A year and a half later, he sold out and retired.

Leaning back in his swivel chair, McMath said he would hate to ever see the sign torn down. "I want it to stay there until the wind blows it down," he said, but quickly added, "Course that'll never happen if it's maintained properly."

Looking back over his career, he decided because of all the Flying Red Horse's magnitude, it's fame and the way it has held up in the face of all the elements, the sign represents his crowning achievement.

In October, 1973, the Dallas City Council lent credence to his belief by declaring the Flying Red Horse a landmark sign, thus protecting it from the restrictions imposed by a new tougher sign ordinance.

McMath doesn't get downtown as much as he used to, but it bothers him that the sign doesn't turn as it was designed to do.

His company maintained the sign until 1961, but he said the Flying Red Horse never did turn consistently after that and now the country's new energy consciousness may make it moot anyway.

Suddenly the old man brightened, "If I were a young man, I could make it turn," he said.

"I got an idea to make that sign turn better than it ever did before. I wouldn't be afraid to stick my neck out and try it. Back then, I wasn't scared of anything."

And just by the look in McMath's eyes and the tone of his voice, you knew he was telling the truth.

Chapter 1:

Perspectives of a Child: J.B.'s Childhood Memories

Prelude: John Bunyan McMath Sr.'s story starts with his inclinations about God at a very early age. He was raised with four siblings and spent most of his childhood in the cities of Marlin, Galveston, and Dallas, Texas. J.B.'s family was typical of the era where children loved their parents, and were content with a simple life. If they were different than other children of their time, it was because their parents were Christians, which for them included living a holy lifestyle. The following early writings are in order by the dates. J.B. Sr. wrote them and they are his own words.

Early Memory Before Leaving Arkansas in 1897

My older brother, Minor, and his cousin Walter Reeves, who was about his same age gathered up all the discarded scrap metal items around the farm one time and built what they called "their play gin." (I'm assuming J.B. meant "cotton gin.") They selected a pine grove a short distance from the front of J.B.'s. Grandfather's house as a perfect place to build it. They cut down small pine saplings, using the trunks to build a fence or pen around their gin that was approximately ten feet square. The branches were used to form what was called a "brush heap" into which they formed a hiding place.

One day Minor and Walter, my sister Nellie, and our cousin Jeffrey Reeves, the oldest of the group, and myself were all sitting inside the pen admiring the junk pile when some one of the group cried out, "Yonder comes Old Lil!" Old Lil was one of grandmother's milk cows that seemed to hate children with a passion, and every child was deathly afraid of her. With the words," Yonder comes Old Lil!" everyone but me jumped out of the pen and made a scramble for the brush heap. Jeffrey happened to look back and see me sitting right where they left me, and he cried, "Oh, we left Bunyan," and rushed out to save me! He lifted me out of the pen and into the brush heap before Lil was close enough to see me. That was my first close encounter with danger in the form of a cow!

Move to Galveston 1899

Prelude: Living in Galveston during this period of time had historical significance because it was shortly before the Great Hurricane of 1900. What follows is J.B Sr's childhood account from the time his family moved to Galveston until they left shortly before the hurricane. Other childhood accounts included are of his earliest memories of living in Dallas over one hundred years ago.

Arrival in Galveston

Our family moved from Marlin to Galveston, Texas in the late Fall of 1899. I was just past five years old. However, I can still remember the trip as if it were only yesterday!

It was pouring rain the night we left Marlin on the old A&TC (now the S.P. railroad), a lovely railroad line that runs from Waco to Bremond where it joins the main line again.

Marlin's famous city marshal Major Coleman used his umbrella to protect us from the rain while we boarded the train, and personally helped me aboard. Regretfully, I witnessed this man assassinated some five or six years later.

I will never forget arriving in Houston the next morning. One of the men in the engine room looked much older than the others so I got the impression that they were father and sons. I thought the oldest man owned the train and his sons were helping him run it.

We arrived at Galveston sometime around noon as I recall and there were two things that impressed me most, one was the long trestle along the bay. I could not see the trestle itself through our coach window so it appeared as though the train itself was running into the water.

The next amazing and somewhat enlightening impression was what I thought to be the end of the railroad. Why I say amazing and enlightening was that I had worried and wondered ever since I had seen my first railroad just where it ended. I was somewhat inclined to believe that the track made a complete circle but was a little skeptical of this theory so naturally it bothered me. I have been very fond of railroads all my life and even now I can be interested in most anything that concerns them. As we emerged from the train my eyes caught sight of the end of the track and I remarked to my child self, "Well, I have found the end of the railroad at last." To me a great mystery had been solved.

Our father had gone to Galveston ahead of us and had already obtained temporary living quarters in a rooming house operated by a widow woman named Mrs. Curly.

Of course, we were all tired and sleepy from our night and part of a day on the train, with the exception of my little brother Dale, so we all lay down for a nap.

After an hour or so Mama awoke to find that Dale was missing and had left the room. This happened within a month of Dale's third birthday and he still remembers it. It was raining when we awoke and naturally the rain added to our fear for Dale's safety. My mother had never lived in such a large city before with so much water, so many people and so many dangerous streetcars, so she almost went into hysterics. Pappa however was more accustomed to the ways of a city, so naturally he was more calm and seemed to know just what to do, and that was to call the police which he did immediately, and it wasn't but a few minutes until we had found Dale only two blocks away where some ladies had taken him in, fed him, and put him to sleep, and by the way, he had already wet the bed!

Our rooming house lady, Mrs. Curly had a nephew about my age living with her and he had the first tricycle I ever rode upon. One day he and I were throwing sand off the paved street in front of the house when a night policeman saw us and chased us in our yard. That was the first Negro policeman I had ever seen.

Mrs. Curly was very careful about her nephew's manner and particularly his English. She would scold him for pointing his finger or for saying, "way out yonder."

We did not live with Mrs. Curly very long until we moved into a small house owned by a Mrs. Swatsburgh who also was a widow. She was an old lady and very childish. She had lost a daughter some time previous to our acquaintance and she could hardly carry on a conversation without mentioning this daughter who she called Lovey and she would always cry. Mrs. Swatsburgh also had a habit of grieving almost incessantly and so loudly that you could hear her at least one hundred feet away. I got to mocking her not to make fun but just to see if I could, and I formed the habit as badly as she had it. We grunted so much alike that my folks could not tell weather it was she or I. My father had quite a time breaking me of this habit. It seemed I was always afflicted in my boyhood days with some kind of a silly habit. One of the worst habits I had while in Galveston was patting my foot, especially at the dining table, and my father would have to threaten to send me away from the table to get me to stop. I had two other habits in those days and one was blinking my eyes and another was spelling incessantly.

Business in my fathers line of work became very dull at this time so he decided to go to Houston and work for a while, letting us remain in Galveston. I mention this incident for one reason in particular and that is because I have in my possession two original letters that my sister Nellie and brother Minor wrote to my father while he was away at that time. Nellie was only seven and a half years old and had never seen inside a school, as in those days you had to be at least eight years old before you could enter a free school. What follows is a copy of the two letters she wrote my father:

Dear Papa,

I will write you a few lines. Bunyan (J.B.'s childhood nickname) and I go down to the beach and me and Nellie draw all the time and Bunyan is drawing a picture. Well, I will close.

Minor McMath

Dear Papa,

I will try to write you a few lines. By this time I was glad to get your letter. Bunyan and Minor go to the beach. They been today. Well, I had not much to write. I will close by this time.

Nellie McMath

A very interesting memory of our stay in the Swatburgh house was a family in back of us who had a parrot that could sing and could whistle "After the Ball is Over" just as good as any human being. He could also say, "Polly wants a cracker," as good as I could say it. I later saw a clipping in the Dallas News that stated an account of an old parrot that could sing and whistle, "After the Ball is Over." It gave the parrot's age at about ninety years. This was without a doubt the same parrot that I had seen and heard over fifty years previously and don't forget he had weathered the 1900 hurricane storm.

We stayed in the Swatburgh house through the winter, and then moved in early spring to a house near the beach, which we shared with a family from Australia named Sneed.

I cannot remember the names of any of the streets we lived on while in Galveston. However, I do remember that this last house was near the end of a street where it dead-ended into the Old Beach Hotel. This hotel had burned down sometime previous to our moving to Galveston and its remains were at the end of our street and very near to our house.

This house belonged to a family name Flcor, they lived in a house in one part of the same lot and I understood they lived through the 1900 flood. On a trip to Galveston several years later I inquired of a former neighbor who had lived in Galveston before and during the great flood as to the street that had dead ended into the Old Beach Hotel before the flood and they informed me that this portion of the Island was completely washed away. In other words this portion of the Island is now out in the Gulf. Our family moved from Galveston to Dallas on June 4, 1900, just exactly three months and four days before the flood and hurricane, which was September eighth of the same year.

A policeman and his family named Swansen lived next door to us and we learned that every member of his family except Mr. Swansen drowned in the hurricane. He happened to be downtown on duty and was saved. We understood that the Sneed family moved back to Australia soon after we left Galveston so their lives were spared. Strange as it may sound, I as only a child felt the whole time we lived in Galveston that something terrible was going to happen. We lived so near the beach that you could hear the roaring of the water day and night and it sounded like some great and ferocious monster that was threatening to attack any minute. As a matter of fact I never enjoyed a single day in that city for fear of impending danger. We had the eclipse of the sun and moon while living there and people were looking at the sun through smoked glass, and it almost frightened me to death, all because of the fear that was already in my heart from the feeling I had of impending calamity.

The Sneed family had two sons; the oldest about my age and his name was Orvol. Mrs. Sneed gave Orval a nickel one day to buy candy with. In those days you could buy as much candy for a nickel as you can buy today for a quarter or more. Naturally we children were very fond of candy for it was seldom that we ever had any because of the scarcity of money in those days. Orval came home with his candy and passed it around to every member of both families except me. Just why he overlooked or slighted me I will never know. However to top it all no one seemed to notice that I had been slighted and even though my heart was breaking and my mouth watering I had too much pride to ask for something that I did not feel perfectly welcome to.

Finally all the children decided to go down to the beach to play and to add to all my insult they did not even invite me to go along. Feeling as I did it is doubtful I would have gone anyway. However, after a half hour or so had transpired I decided to take a stroll all alone and with my heavy heart and dejected soul I started towards the front gate, and just as I approached the gate I spied an old, darkened nickel right beside the pathway. No doubt the nickel had been walked over a hundred times and perhaps a thousand times without anyone noticing it. This nickel was of the old type with a shield on one side and the figure "J" on the other.

Of course my crushed spirit was revived immediately and I lit out for the candy store where we bought most of our candy in those days and bought a big sack of my favorite candy. By this time I had changed my mind about not going to the beach, and I decided to go immediately so Orval in particular could see my candy. So I rushed down and finally corralled the gang and then passed my candy around to everyone except Orval and to my delight he began to bawl. However his crying was short lived as my sister Nellie, who was the oldest of the group by two years, divided her portion with Orval, so he was satisfied. This little story might sound childish and not worth recording but to me it is one of the most cherished memories of my entire life and that for the simple reason that I believe with all of my heart that God or one of his angels directed me to that old nickel. Never in my life had a nickel meant so much. No one but God and my self will ever understand what it meant to my childish heart. However I doubt the Lord led me to provoke Orval by refusing to give him some of my candy. I might have shown a better spirit by offering to divide with him even though he did not give me any of his candy. The Lord says to do good even to your enemies and to those who disrespectfully use you. In this way you make them ashamed of their misdeeds and will hopefully cause them to repent.

My father used to go fishing or oyster gathering when he did not have work to do. He would usually catch all the fish we could eat and have some to sell, and believe it or not you could sell all the fish you could catch right there to the people living within two blocks of the gulf where anyone could catch them. Occasionally he would go up to the bay near where the railroad crossed it and get oysters. He would usually bring home a yellow bucket full and already shelled. As to fruit I recall that papa could buy a large bunch of bananas for 25 cents at the wharf. There are still two old landmarks in

Galveston that are familiar to my boyhood memories and they are the old fire station in the long, narrow building downtown. I believe it was Metro Station and it is still there. The other landmark is the large statue. My father told us the history of this statue and the name of the man who gave it to the city. I returned to Galveston for the first time after the 1900 flood in 1916 with a group of young men who had never been there before and as I stepped off the train in the same direction and it all came back to me immediately, and I was able to direct our entire tour of Galveston. Going to the wharf first and then on to the beach, the Sea Wall of course changed the appearance of the beach but the directions were not the least bit confusing.

About this time, my mother's brother Uncle Warren Reeves had just moved to Dallas from Columbia, Texas and he persuaded my father to move to Dallas. This decision most likely saved the lives of our entire family as we just missed the flood by three months and four days as before mentioned and where we last lived was completely washed away.

We were living in Galveston when several shiploads of our sailors from the Spanish American War stopped over for several days on their way home.

As strange as it may seem I do not remember the day we left Galveston for Dallas. However I do remember arriving at Dallas. Our father had gone ahead as usual and prepared living quarters for us and I remember he met our train, the old H & T.C. with its depot, and then the T & P railroad brought us to Elm Street. Papa bought us a lunch consisting mainly of warm bread. I also remember that Mamma went immediately upon arrival to the bedside of Uncle Warren Reeves accompanied by Aunt Nancy who was sick with the measles and from which she did not recover. The house she died in was on the east side and adjacent to the old No. 2 Fire Station at Commerce and Hawkins St. This house was still standing when I came back to Dallas in 1917. We lived in several different houses the short time we stayed in Dallas. The one I remember best was next to the little H. & T.C. Park at Commerce Street and the Central Railroad. It was a little two-story house and our back fence separated us from the Brooke Carriage Shoppe. This shop was still operating and in the same location when I came back to

Dallas in 1917. The house on our east side was on the corner of Hawkins and Mr. Charley Caufman, a fireman, lived there. He worked at the fire station across the street known as Engine Company No. 2. Mr. Caufman became chief of the Dallas Fire Department for a short while several years later. I saw him several times before he died. I used to go over to the station and slide down the pole when I was six years old.

The Dallas Fair was going on during our stay in this house and there were many tractors and various vehicles that passed our house going to the fairgrounds. I recall walking out to the grounds one day during the fair and as I remember there was a board across the front entrance similar to a country ballpark with all the area directly in front of the fairgrounds and toward the Santa Fe yards an open place. There were all kinds of covered eating-places in this area.

I had hunted pecans and crawfished all up and down the old area that used to run under Commerce Street near where a plant is now located. My brother and I were gathering pecans from a branch one day and a man came along who made us divide our pecans with him.

I can remember standing on Main Street one day and seeing Bill Cody's "Buffalo Bill and his Wild West Show Parade." Last year I saw a picture in the Dallas Chamber of Commerce Magazine of Buffalo Bill taken at the very same time spot some fifty-three years later.

My father took my oldest brother and sister Minor and Nellie and myself on top of the courthouse one Sunday to see the sights. I recall we had to climb a ladder a part of the way. This was long before they removed the steeple from the top of the structure because of its unsafe condition. This was the highest structure in Dallas at that time (three stories) and if my memory serves me right there was a clock and a large bell on the courthouse at that time for it seems to me that I heard the clock striking while we were up there.

My father was a house painter as well as a sign painter and all of the professional pictures that we had made of the family during this time were in partial payment by some photographer for painting or sign services. We had at least three family group pictures that we purchased in this manner.

There was one taken of us children while we lived in Dallas and I remember on our way to the photographer's studio that I picked up a little frog and held it in my hand while the picture was taken. I still have a copy of the picture.

My father while in Dallas ran a carriage paint shop upstairs above the House Blacksmith Shop on I believe Commerce Street somewhere near the Adolphus Hotel. Soon after my father took over this carriage paint shop the city of Dallas had a fire wagon they wanted painted and it happened that no one in Dallas wanted to take the job but my father and he did such a beautiful job that he received many compliments. Mr. House that owned the blacksmith shop, and later invented the Haus Scrubber (that was a tool that all old blacksmiths are familiar with), complimented my father.

Dallas had a population of only about 50,000 at this time, about 1900. There used to be a little Baptist Church somewhere just off of Main Street that I attended when a child. I will never forget our iceman, a Mr. White was the Sunday School Superintendent and I thought he was the best man in the world. Grown people should be very careful how they conduct themselves around children as many times they make a good or bad impression that stays with a child for life. This man was so kind and saintly and seemed to know just what to say or do to make you feel good. I recall one day while I was in the Sunday school that another little boy noticed that I was not singing. The reason I wasn't singing was that I didn't know any of the songs and naturally I could not read at that age and he brought it to the attention of Mr. White and he says, "Well, that is all right, he is just doing fine anyway so you can just keep singing yourself and don't bother about him." The kind and truthful way he handled the little situation gave me a great admiration for the man that I never forgot.

Columbia County Arkansas 1905-1906: Money Grows on Trees

Members of my family, including myself, while the age of eleven, spent several months in Columbia County Arkansas from late fall 1905 until early spring 1906.

One day after we moved back to our home in Marlin, Texas I was telling a boy friend of mine who was about two years younger than I, about all the wonders of Arkansas, that any kind of fruits and nuts he might wish for could be found growing wild in the woods, and about the abundance of fish and game. In fact, I made it seem like the Garden of Eden.

In the meantime I kept my eye upon him, in order to detect if possible any signs of doubt about the truth of what I was telling him, and detected none, but to the contrary he seemed to accept everything with such enthusiasm, that I desired to make it just a little stronger, so I told him that even money grew on trees in Arkansas, and that they didn't even pick up the pennies, but just let them lay where they fell. He said nothing for several minutes after I had finished this time, I thought I had gone too far and ruined my whole story. But, after a few minutes he says, "Bunyan, if you ever go to Arkansas again please send me a shoe box full of those pennies."

Minor Warren McMath.

Chapter Two:

God Comes Calling

The first person in the McMath family to have a relationship with the living God was Bunyan's brother, Minor. I include this letter because it was Minor's conversion to Christ that began to stir up the things of God in the life of J.B. McMath and eventually the rest of his family. The following letter Minor wrote to his family after his conversion to Jesus Christ. It was written on March 9, 1915 from Dallas, Texas. The letter is in his own words.

Dear Mama, Papa, and all,

I am out of practice at writing letters, it has been so long since I wrote to anyone but I must write you all tonight and tell of my wonderful experience last night for it concerns me more than anything else now and I pray that what I am going to say to you will be believed by you and that you will also receive the blessing. Yes, a blessing-one of the greatest blessings that man can receive.

For a long time I have been deeply concerned about my salvation –in fact that is really the cause of my long silence to you all, but glory to God I don't have to worry about it now for there is an absolute assurance, without a shadow of a doubt that we are on our way to heaven (we meaning Ethel (his wife) and Minor). Yes, she has been blessed too and I am so thankful to God that I was given such an agreeable companion to accompany me through this temporal life, but what is even greater is that she shall accompany me to eternal life.

I am a different being now, dear parents—the world looks brighter—however I have lost all desire for the things of this world and all I seek is to know more about God and to get closer and closer to him.

You remember, mama, when I was at home last spring I talked to you about how I would like to be where I could attend some little, lowly country or suburban church and fellowship with a humble, poor, common class of Christians. My heart ached for that and at times I would almost despair of ever seeing a true Christian to know it, and a few times I would all but forsake the Lord, consequently I was very unhappy and even miserable at times. I continued to be that way until recently. But now I am happy and contented and am praising God that I realized the truth in the verse: "Blessed are they that hunger and thirst after righteousness for they shall be filled."

Let me tell you, there are thousands of church members and churchgoers and even Christians that don't know anything about serving God. Ethel and I started going to the Central Congregational Church and were attending regularly but when I began to feel that I was still just doing the same old thing and my desires hadn't been filled, I lost interest and so did Ethel and we just quit going. But just before Christmas Mr. Aaron Pickett, the fine workman you have heard me speak of so much that was working for Borich when I first came to Dallas, came over from Ft. Worth to work for Borich again and is our foreman now. He used to be a wild fellow, has a wife and two older children, but used to drink and smoked all the time and cursed and was very wicked when I first knew him. But you should see him now.

Perhaps you have already heard of the Apostolic faith before now. The devil has invented a new name for it however and the people are laughed at and made fun of as the "Holy Rollers" because when they first commenced holding meetings under tents a few years ago they taught and preached that God would heal the sick and cause the people to talk in unknown tongues today just the same as he did in Christ's time or rather just after Christ's ascension. It was the Holy Ghost that came in and took control of a man's tongue and filled him with power and Christ taught that he had to first ascend to the Father before the Comforter, as he called the Holy Ghost, would be sent to the apostles. The word says that "they were in accord constantly praising God" when they were filled with the Holy Ghost and were caused to speak languages unknown to themselves. That is just what you must do today to receive it and it is nothing to hear different people praying and praising God in all kinds of strange languages at all of their meetings.

But what I started to say was that the power of the Spirit would overcome sinners sometimes and they would speak in unknown tongues. Sometimes they would fall down and roll on the ground, hence the term "Holy Rollers."

Mr. Pickett became an Apostolic about two years ago after he and his wife had been drawing straws to see which place they would go to have the most fun, the picture show or the tent "theatre." He had even went so far before as to say that those people should be run out of town (the Pentecostals). But he went to church one time too many for the devil and his lost condition was pictured so clearly in his mind that he couldn't resist, despite the protest of his wife, and he went down to the altar at church and stayed on his knees from 9:30 to 12:00 and got all of his sins forgiven, received the Holy Ghost, talked in unknown tongues, and went away a new man. He was "born again" with all desire for tobacco, booze, and every other worldly desire swept clean and he has been that way ever since. He can pray one of the most powerful prayers ever uttered, and not because of large vocabulary or skillful use of language, but because the Holy Ghost prays through him according to the will of God.

Well, when Mr. Pickett got to telling me about his religion and church and I knew that was just what my heart had desired for so long and I finally attended one of their cottage meetings held at his house (of which they have at several different houses six nights in the week). Ethel was with me and we got interested and the following Sunday I went out to their church, Ethel had to stay at home on account of her mother being sick. His home was a low box house with a flat roof and sawdust for a floor with a row of small windows clear around the top of the walls and plain benches to sit on but God was certainly there and I got terribly worked up and went to the altar with Mr. Pickett and partook of the sacraments. Then I went another

Sunday and always went to the altar seeking the baptism of the Holy Ghost. Last Sunday week I went by myself in the morning and felt the Holy Spirit but weakened before I prayed through and I gave up praying after being on my knees for quite a while. That night I made another try and failed but Ethyl received the Holy Ghost and talked a little in an unknown tongue. I was too busy praying and being prayed for that I didn't know what she was doing but I know that she is very happy and is getting happier every day. I didn't give up and we went out last night and went to the altar both times but failed to receive the baptism in the Holy Spirit. However, I still had hopes and intended to keep trying. A lady (Mrs. Sherrell) invited us out to a prayer meeting last night telling Ethel that her husband would surely receive the baptism if I came out there, so we went there last night. They had a nice little crowd. Mr. Pickett was present and after singing a few hymns and listening to a few readings about the importance of all Christians receiving the Holy Ghost we all got down on our knees and began to pray and to praise the Lord with uplifted hands and faces. I wrestled and tusseled with the Holy Spirit and about despaired of receiving it and finally Mr. Pickett came over to my side and told all of the Christians to get together in one accord and pray me through. Let me tell you when a few are gathered together in the name of the Lord something is going to happen and they hadn't been around me for more than a few seconds before I arose to my feet and began to praise God in different languages. I started off with the words "glory to God" but as soon as the Holy Spirit came in I lost control of my tongue and the praises from my heart were uttered in just the words and language that God chose-I talked for more than half an hour and spoke at least four or five different languages. I myself and others recognized Chinese and Hebrew, and I want to tell you that was the happiest moment of my life and I have felt as light as a feather ever since. I am just as sure of my salvation as I am that I am writing this letter and I am going to pray for you all and sincerely trust that you will believe what I am telling you as you always have believed me.

 I know that there is only one true and living God with whom all things are possible and that he sent his only begotten Son to die for our sins and that all, absolutely all, that is required of anyone is to believe that Jesus Christ died and paid the price for our sins and be saved. Then work out your salvation or "live" it and, keep the commandments. Even though your sins be as scarlet, he will make you whiter than snow. Remember Mary Magdalene.

Now my eyes are getting heavy and I must go to bed. We shall attend another meeting tomorrow night. I will try to write you again soon and tell you all I know-but I am all overcome now with my wonderful experience. You should thank God that you are poor for in that condition you are more able to live for Him for you haven't much between you. Nothing must come between us and God if we want eternal life. We must forsake all. The things of this world look as cheap as dirt to me now. I would have a fortune just long enough to give it away is all and thank God Ethel is "in the same boat." " The Lord is my Shepherd, I shall not want."

People who think that a Christian life means to deprive yourself of all pleasures don't know a thing about it. I am far happier doing the will of God and have absolutely no desire for shows or style or society or any of the worldly pleasures that I used to take part in. Glory to God! Now I must close hoping to hear from you soon.

May God's blessing rest upon you all and may you all come to realize the power of God soon, is my prayer.

Love to all,

Minor

Be sure that this letter is read to every member of the family.

Ethel sends her love and will write soon.

This letter was followed by another dated July 26, 1916

Well, it is now Wednesday night and I will try to finish this letter. I don't know much to write either. Ethel and I are so anxious to get moved and go to house keeping again, and to have you all up here with us. Things are getting disagreeable for us (especially for Ethel) here where we are boarding and I am awfully sorry too for it keeps me bothered a little bit and I know that we should not worry about anything. Don't forget to pray that the Lord will deliver us and that we can be to ourselves in peace.

Bunyan, I want you to press on and don't let anything or anybody disturb your religion-you are saved regardless of your feelings if you have forsaken your sins and believe in the Lord Jesus Christ and are confessing Him to the world. Your interest in religious affairs and in the Bible and your attitude toward sin and the devil and the unusual temptations and testing that you are having, all go to prove that you have repented. Repentance is to change your mind about things and to turn from your own ideas and your own ways and accept God's way: that's repentance. Now you must just keep on exercising your will power to do the will of God as far as you understand it and to stand on God's promises, feeling or no feeling. I'll tell you I can't afford to depend on my feelings anymore but just the same I know that I am saved all the time because the word of God says so whether I feel like it or not. I know that I would not commit any kind of a sin if I knew it and I know that Jesus Christ died to save me and that he arose for my justification. I have accepted Him as my Savior and the Lord of my life and have made up my mind to step right out on all of his promises feeling or no feeling because they are His promises and are certainly true. Jesus said, "For whosoever shall do the will of God the same is my brother and my sister, and my mother." Mark 3:35. He didn't say anything about whosoever is happy or has had a blessing is my brother, etc. but "Whosoever shall do the will of God." And again Jesus said, "Verily, Verily, I say unto you, He that heareth my word and believeth on Him that sent me, hath everlasting life, and shall not come in to condemnation; but is passed from death unto life." James 5:24. And again Jesus said, "My doctrine is not mine, but His that sent me; If any man will do His will, he shall know of the doctrine, whether it be of God; or whether I speak of myself." John 7: 6, 17. All the way through the Bible we can see that salvation was not by our feelings. Men didn't depend on feelings and they didn't seek for feelings to know about the condition of their souls, but just put their will into it and just say, "I will believe God," "I will trust God," "I will obey Him," "I will keep his commandments." Jesus said, "If any man will do the will of God, he shall know," and I'll tell you that no man ever started out to do the will of God and kept at it from an unselfish standpoint, but because it was the right thing to do, that sooner or later was not overtaken with a blessing.

We must not seek for blessings, but to do the will of God. When God sees that we mean what we say and will keep faithful we won't be able to contain his blessings. They will flow through us as streams of living water-we will bubble over with joy-that's what makes some people shout-it has to come out after we get so full.

When I say I will believe God, that is all I can do, and I will prove it by stepping out on all his promises and claiming all His benefits through Jesus Christ. If I believe, I am justified and am a brother to the Lord Jesus Christ, a child of God and a just heir with Jesus Christ to all that God has in his whole creation. He says, "All that I have is Thine." "And this is the confidence that we have in Him, that if we ask anything according to His will he heareth us." 1 John 5:14. God says, "Bring ye all the tithes (a tenth part of your earnings; and also your opportunities to do or to pray and to do all that you can for His glory, is what is meant by the tithes) into the storehouse, that there may be meat in mine house, and prove me now herewith, saith the Lord of hosts, if I will not open you the windows of heaven and pour you out a blessing, that there shall not be room enough to contain it." Malachi 3:10.

Man was created a free moral agent and the will of a man is the part of the man that God cannot control because it would be against His plan and furthermore would be no source of pleasure or satisfaction to him.

It is only through the exercise of a man's will power that he can please God at all, and of course we are pleasing him only to the extent in which we will do his will, or exercise our will (or ourselves) in harmony with His will.

Now, I have an idea that you are likely to say to yourself that you are willing and will do those things all right, "but what about my heart, and what about the first and greatest commandment that "Thou shalt love the Lord thy God with all thy heart, and with all thy soul, and mind, and strength"-how can I do that"? Can I just will to do that too? The heart as it is mentioned in the Bible means (not your old heart of flesh) but it means a man's inmost being-the center of life-in reality it is the man himself-the same as a man's will-Therefore to love God with all your heart is the same thing as loving Him with all your will power-which is all that God expects of any person.

Well, you say, I don't feel like I love God like I should. I say never mind the feeling, that is God's part of the transaction. "For this is the love of God that we keep his commandments." 1 John 5:3 "Well, you say, what about being born again?' "Jesus says that we must be born again!" Jesus said right-but that part of it is not your business at all-that is God's business-you never mind about that end of it, but keep striving to do the whole will of God and you won't die disappointed by any means. Furthermore, you very likely have already been born of the Spirit of Christ and don't know it because you haven't been blessed just like you expected to be. How do you know but what you were born again the night you dreamed of being saved? God is very likely, and no doubt in my mind, just trying out your faithfulness and allowing you to walk altogether by faith. All Christians have that experience. So, by all means with faithful feeling or no feeling I will guarantee that God will pour out such a blessing on you that before long you won't have room to contain it.

Be definite and determined and sincere with God because He doesn't like lukewarmness nor indifference, for if He loved this old sinful world enough to send His only Son to die for us that we might live, why naturally He expects us to be anything else but indifferent in regard to that matter.

Make a special effort every day to do something for the Lord, tell a friend about Him, speak a word in His favor, exalt Him continually in your heart and with your lips and "Let your moderation be made known unto all men" Philippians 4:5. But most of all pray, pray, pray, "Men ought always to pray and not faint." "Pray without ceasing." 1 Thess. 5:17. And "study to show thyself approved unto God, a workman that needeth not to be ashamed, rightly dividing the word of truth." 2 Tim. 2:15. "And if any man lack wisdom, let him ask of God, that giveth to all men liberally and upbraideth not and it shall be given him. James 1:5.

Now, Bunyan, I could go on and on repeating good scriptures to you but, go to your Bible and you will find the whole thing. Study it and ask God to explain it to you. The New Testament is the best for you to study first and especially the gospel of Saint John and then the epistles of Paul to the different churches and to Timothy especially. Then the epistles of Peter, James, John and Jude.

Now I must close and go to bed. Let me hear from you all soon, and pray for us.

May the Lord bless this letter to your soul and He shall have the praise.

Love to all,

Minor

After reading this letter it is an appropriate time to share from J.B.'s own hand his experience with Jesus Christ after his brother Minor had his experience.

The Testimony of J.B. McMath, Sr.

As strange as it may seem to some, the Lord began dealing with my life while I was at the age of five years and two months. He continued to deal with me, without my knowing it was He, until my conversion some sixteen years and six months later; therefore, I would not consider my testimony complete without my relating at least some of the incidents with definite spiritual implications.

Not until my conversion to Christ was I made to understand that God no doubt had had a hand in those seemingly mysterious experiences which occurred in my life before my conversion. All of these things taught me some good lessons, and they have enhanced and inspired my faith in God and His infallible word.

Now there may be those who will doubt the validity of some of the experiences which I will relate, all because of my young age at the time of their occurrence.

Please do not think I am classifying myself with the prophet Samuel when I give him as an example of God's dealing with children. In the third chapter of First Samuel, when Samuel was only six years old, the Lord gave him a prophecy concerning judgment upon the house of the high priest Eli for the wickedness of his two sons.

Jesus used a child to exemplify the attributes with which every Christian should be endowed. Matthew 18:2-3: "And Jesus called a little child unto him, and set him in the midst of them. And said, Verily, I say unto you, except ye be converted, and become as little children, ye shall not enter into the kingdom of heaven." Now if Jesus would use little children as examples of what true Christians should be like, is there any reason not to believe that He would speak to them at times as well?

I am just as convinced that God spoke to my heart many times long before my conversion as I am that He has spoken to my heart many times since my conversion. There is no doubt many Christians who, if they would think about it, could remember incidents in their lives which they took for granted, or considered incidental, but now, since becoming a Christian, they can recognize the hand of God in many of those incidents.

Our family, consisting of father, mother, and five children, moved from Marlin to Galveston, Texas in early November 1899. I was only five years and two months of age at this time, and I cannot remember before moving to Galveston, of ever hearing the words cyclone, hurricane, or flood mentioned; they simply were not in my vocabulary.

We had no more than settled in Galveston when I was seized with a dreadful fear which turned out to be a premonition of the great 1900 hurricane and flood which all but destroyed Galveston and caused the greatest loss of life of any peacetime disaster in American history up until that time. Everything I looked upon seemed to be artificial or temporary, nothing permanent or secure.

While I was not aware of what I feared, nevertheless I very definitely believed that Galveston was going to suffer a great disaster of some kind. My greatest concern was that our family might be there when the disaster occurred. This fear never left me until we boarded the train to leave Galveston for Dallas on June 4, 1900. It was not until three months later, when the great hurricane and flood struck, that I was made to understand what I had feared.

In the late 1920's I took my wife and children to Galveston for a brief vacation. While there we stopped at the Hawkins Tourist Lodge on a prominent corner of the seawall. A young Mr. Hawkins managed the lodge and his elderly father acted more or less as a goodwill ambassador.

One day while there I informed young Mr. Hawkins that I had once lived in Galveston, but had moved away just prior to the great 1900 disaster, and I would appreciate it if he could direct me to someone who could show me where I had lived. I could not remember the name of the street, but I could describe its location well enough that anyone familiar with Galveston could show it to me.

Mr. Hawkins replied, "My father has lived in Galveston all of his years, even through the flood, and can tell you anything you may wish to know about Galveston." Therefore, my wife and I went to the elderly Mr. Hawkins and told him everything I had told his son. I informed him that we had lived on the last street that ran parallel to the Gulf, where it dead-ended at the site of the old Beach Hotel. With this he paused several seconds, as though astonished, and then quietly said, "That spot now is just exactly two blocks out in the Gulf. That much of the island was washed into the sea."

He asked if I remembered the car line that ran parallel to the beach. I replied, "Yes, the car line was the only thing between us and the Gulf." He then said, "Not an item of that car line was ever recovered after the storm."

This will give you some idea of what would have become of our entire family had it not been for the providence of our God. It is estimated that between seven and eight thousand people perished during the hurricane. Few people other than those who witnessed this tragedy and are still alive are able to know how serious, murderous and devastating were the effects upon Galveston and its citizens.

In concluding this portion of my testimony, I wish to quote two paragraphs of a letter written by Clara Barton, president and founder of the American Red Cross at Philadelphia. She was in Galveston administering first aid at the time. I quote: "The conditions here are as much as you will gather from what you have read. Like some other fields that we have visited, it does not admit of exaggeration. One can scarcely imagine how it could have been worse, and yet one sees the city full of people left alive; but when we think of the hundreds, and it may even be thousands, lying buried and decaying in great heaps of debris which are stretched for miles along the edge of what was once a town, it is hard to conjecture anything worse.

This city will be built again, probably finer than before, and it was a fine city always, but I hope never without a protection from the storms. It is critical to allow people, perfectly unsuspecting, to settle themselves and live on territory, however beautiful, that is morally certain at some evil moment to cause destruction.

This statement from Clara Barton expresses my feelings about the destruction of Galveston better than I could have worded it myself.

As before mentioned, our family moved from Galveston to Dallas in early June, 1900, and remained there until early spring of 1901, at which time we moved back to Marlin. Now in late fall of 1902, I was seized again with a premonition and dreadful fear, which lasted until we moved away from the house we were then living in, in the early spring of 1903.

I was now eight years old, and mature enough to know what I feared, and that was a cyclone. With every dark cloud that arose, every flash of lightening, and every clap of thunder, I looked for a cyclone. Since I knew what I feared, I confided my feelings to my mother. She would always give me the same logic; namely, "Don't you know we have had dark clouds, flashes of lighting, and claps of thunder since the beginning of creation, and always will have?" But that answer did not change my opinions or soothe my feelings.

Two weeks to the day after we moved from that house, and while eating breakfast one morning, a man knocked at our door and, when we invited him in, he asked if we had heard what happened to the house we had vacated a few days ago? We replied, "No." He said, "A cyclone blew it away this morning."

A neighbor living nearby said he heard the roaring of the wind and rushed to his front porch just in time to see our former house leave the ground, in a few seconds disintegrating as though it had exploded.

The storm occurred without warning, and would have found every member of our family either in bed or up preparing for breakfast. The chances of any member of our family surviving would have been just as unlikely as would have been our chances of surviving the hurricane should we have remained in Galveston.

One of the most peculiar things about this storm was that our former house was the only one in the city to be destroyed. There was a house close to that house on one side and another directly in front of it, neither of which was even scratched. The storm just simply dipped down and lifted our former house from its foundation, as was seen by our former neighbor from his front porch.

Our next experience of note occurred in the summer of 1906, just before my twelfth birthday, when a Spirit-filled father and son named Bell from Waco came to my hometown (Marlin) for a series of street meetings. It is whom the elder Bell later became that makes this brief story interesting.

Their first presentation was the father's personal testimony. He began it by saying, "I was a saloon keeper in Waco, and became sick unto death. I knew I was going to die. I promised God if he would let me live, I would get out of the saloon business, and give Him the remainder of my life. He not only healed me, but He saved both my son and me and baptized each of us in the Holy Ghost, and we are now preaching the gospel."

While there were no doubt many converts, from what I have observed of the full gospel message over the years, I cannot remember them preaching anything contrary to sound full gospel doctrine, with possibly one exception. The second coming of Christ was not generally taught in those days; therefore, instead of preaching the soon coming of Christ, as we do today, they taught that the world was soon coming to an end, and they were not far wrong at that, for wicked men's rule of this world will surely end when Jesus comes back to rule in righteousness.

Many of the old-timers in the Assemblies of God will remember the late, prominent E.L. Bell, who was one of the principal organizers of what is now known as the Assemblies of God Fellowship, at Hot Springs, Arkansas, on April 2-12, 1914, and for his tireless prayers and persistent efforts in its consummation. He was elected its first chairman in 1914 and again in 1919 through 1923.

One day in 1975, while meditating upon the Bells' Marlin meeting, some sixty-nine years later, the question suddenly came to mind: Is it possible that the elder Bell whom I had heard preach at Marlin in 1906 is the same Bell who was so prominent in the Assemblies of God Fellowship, especially in the early days? Therefore I called my pastor, the Rev. E.M. Fjordbak, who has been an Assembly of God minister over thirty-five years, and is a graduate of Central Bible Institute (as it was known then), and asked if he knew any of the background of the late Rev. E.N. Bell. He replied, "Yes, I surely do." I asked him where Brother Bell was from. He replied, "Waco, Texas." I then asked him if he had been a saloon keeper and Pastor Fjordbak replied, "Yes, he was a saloon keeper."

Now this series of events means that I had the pleasure of hearing an outstanding Christian gentleman, Rev. E. N. Bell, preach on the streets of Marlin in 1906, when I was only twelve years old, and the Rev. Bell was a brand-new Christian. This affords me a great pleasure, and is a very fond lifetime memory.

After the Bells left Marlin, it was some nine years later before I met anyone who had experienced contact of any nature with the living God. I grew up to work and associate with people of many faiths and walks of life without ever meeting anyone who could tell me anything about God. I was like a sheep whom had been left with the wolves and, as a result, I drifted into unbelief until I became practically an infidel.

However, the God who had been with me from my early childhood was still with me, even during all this period of gross unbelief. Hardly a day passed that I did not sigh and say, "Wouldn't it be wonderful to know that the Bible is true and heaven is real?" But then I would sigh again and say, "It can't be true, for it is only a myth, or imagination."

My surroundings being void of any spiritual environment or fellowship, I naturally grew more worldly and farther from God, yet I never lost my hunger for truth and reality. However, by the time I had found reality in a Spirit-filled brother, I had grown so worldly that I was not ready to surrender my life to the Lord.

I had a brother named Minor, four years older than myself, who had moved to Dallas in 1912. In early February 1915, he was saved in a Pentecostal church, and on March 8th, one month later, he received the baptism of the Holy Spirit. The day following his baptism he wrote the family at Marlin an eleven-page letter, outlining in detail his glorious salvation and Holy Spirit baptism experience. His beautiful, meek spirit and God-given love just about captivated the family and nine of the ten members of our family eventually became Christians as a result.

On his trip home he confided two dreams he had received recently concerning me. In the first dream he thought he came to Marlin to visit the family and, when he arrived at our house, he heard someone at the rear of the house singing, so he decided to enter through the back door and see whom it was who was singing. He said it was I that I was standing over a washtub and rub board, and that hanging on the clothesline were the most beautiful white clothes he had ever seen. He said he had definitely accepted the dream as being from God, and that it indicated God was going to save me, and that I was going to be a soul winner.

The second dream, which occurred a week later, saw me in a golden ripe harvest field, again all alone and singing, while gathering the grain. We accepted this dream to be a confirmation of his interpretation of the first dream.

My brother was so convinced that these dreams were God-given and would come to pass that he prayed for me approximately fourteen months, until I was saved in April 1916.

You may recall the two dreams which Joseph interpreted for King Pharoah of Egypt, both depicted differently, but identical in meaning, and Joseph said to Pharoah in Genesis 41:32, "And for that the dream was double unto Pharoah twice, it is because the thing is established by God, and God will shortly bring it to pass." Now our two dreams, though different in appearance, but identical in purpose or meaning, lends credence to their divine or spiritual origin, and to their sure fulfillment.

Those two dreams were given in March 1915, and the same month in which my brother received the Holy Spirit baptism, and approximately fourteen months before my conversion to Christ, in the latter part of April 1916, and it was some 45 years after my conversion before I was suddenly aware that my life had been their fulfillment.

I was attending a class on soul winning in 1962, under the tutorship of a minister. It was part of the procedure that each student recite or relate some religious experience which might be of interest to the class. I gave the account of my brother's dream relating to me, and it was at that instant that the Lord revealed to my heart for the first time that those dreams were being fulfilled literally in my life.

As you will recall, both dreams also depicted me all alone and singing, a perfect illustration of my nature. Ninety percent of everything I have ever accomplished for the Lord since I became a Christian has been accomplished while I was alone—but not alone as far as God was concerned, for I have always prayed to Him and He has never failed me. Bless His holy name! As far as singing is concerned, there isn't anything that blesses my soul more than good sacred songs sung in the spirit.

In late February 1916, while working in Marlin's only fire station, I had a day off, and three other young men and myself went down to what was known as the Hot Well Pavilion, to talk and fellowship. One of the young men had been to a doctor that week for physical examination, and the doctor had found him suffering serious effects from the use of tobacco. He admonished the young man to rid himself of the habit, or it could even kill him.

I was greatly impressed with what the doctor told him about tobacco and the health hazards those who persisted in using it encountered. I was a tobacco user of long standing. I chewed tobacco like a goat and smoked cigars when I could afford them, and I thought I had every symptom the doctor mentioned. The other two men were impressed also and both resolved to quit as soon as they used up what they had in their pockets. One of them turned to me and said, "Bunyan, how about joining us?"

I was evidently more impressed than they were, for I took my tobacco from my pocket and pitching it in the street, I spoke the following words as I threw it away, "I will never, as long as I live, let another crumb of tobacco, in any shape, form, or fashion touch my lips." These words must have been put in my mouth by the Spirit of God, for they were too poetic and too extemporaneously spoken to have come from me.

Now God had a hand in this entire affair, as it was very definitely an answer to prayer, as we will see later. However, since I was not a Christian at the time, I did not look upon my deliverance from tobacco as a miracle from God, but thought it was the result of super willpower. I seemed to be impressed with the thought that I had quit tobacco forever. I had never had an experience prior to this one that gave me as much pride and satisfaction in believing I had developed the maturity and willpower to make such an important decision. I could hardly wait for daylight to come so I could start telling my friends I had finally quit tobacco.

I went back to my job at the fire station the next morning. Our first morning chore was to bring our horses out front to a hitching post for their morning currying and grooming. We had a prominent citizen in those days who came by the station quite often to play dominoes and he always smoked a big cigar. To my knowledge he never had, prior to this morning, offered anyone of us a cigar.

This gentleman happened to come by this morning while I was grooming my horses and, in a very friendly voice said, "Good morning, Mack!" to which I replied, "Good morning, sir!" He reached in his top outside pocket and took out a cigar and said, "Here, Mack, have a cigar."

Now even though I did not know God at the time, a still small voice nevertheless spoke to my heart and said, "This is the devil tempting you with that cigar." Therefore, I thanked the man and informed him I had quit tobacco, to which he replied, "Oh? Congratulations!"

After grooming my horses, I put them back in their stalls and went next door where there was a carpenter shop in which two elderly craftsmen were employed. I greatly admired them because of their outstanding skills. My mission for going was to tell them that I had quit tobacco, feeling they surely would be happy for me and would at least congratulate me for my courageous decision.

However, when I said, "Gentlemen, I have quit tobacco," the first one said, "Boy, you can't quit tobacco; you have been using it too long and you will want it just as badly a year from today as you do today." The other one said, "Not only that, but you will lose all your teeth. I tried quitting once and within a year I had to start using it again to save my teeth. The same will happen to you.

My brother in Dallas had not been informed of my having quit the tobacco habit. However, six weeks following the day I quit, he paid us a visit in Marlin, which lasted two weeks. One of the first things I did was to tell him I had quit tobacco, naturally expecting him to shout for joy. Instead of shouting, he just paused for a few seconds as though he were afraid I was not going to like what he had to tell me.

He said, "I was well aware of your addiction to the tobacco habit and was concerned that, should you ever come to Dallas and meet some of my new-found Christian friends, some unwise one might inform you that you would have to give up that tobacco before you could be saved, and it might be a stumbling block to your salvation." "And, " he said, "I asked the church at Dallas to pray that the Lord would deliver my brother at Marlin of the tobacco habit."

This naturally took the wind out of my sails, when I learned it was God and prayer that had delivered me from tobacco and not my own willpower. My brother was not the least surprised to find me free of tobacco. In fact, he said he would have been greatly surprised if he had found me still using it.

He ended his two week visit and prepared to leave for Dallas. I went home from the station and had an early evening meal with him and walked him to the depot. On the way to the depot we had to pass a small house that had stood vacant for months. Today there was a man, his wife and three children on the front porch, making the most beautiful willow lawn settees and chairs I had ever seen, quite a fad in those days.

I accompanied my brother until he boarded the train for Dallas, then went back to the fire station. At about 7:30 I went into my room to prepare my bed for the night, and the instant I entered my room I was seized with such Holy Ghost conviction (John 16:8, "And when he is come, he will reprove the world of sin, and of righteousness, and of judgment.") that I could almost feel it in the atmosphere. I was made to know for the first time in my life that I was a lost soul and on my way to hell. Satan's presence was so real that I trembled with fear that I might visibly see him in my room at any moment, but I never did.

I began to ask myself incessantly, "What must I do to be saved?" These were the exact words the Philippian jailer spoke to Paul and Silas when he recognized his need of God (Acts 16:30, "And brought them out, and said, Sirs, what must I do to be saved?) I was then reminded that Jesus Christ was the living Savior and, at that instant, the echo of beautiful, sacred music began to fill my room and I grabbed my cap and made my way out to see where the music was coming from. One block away, on a corner in front of a saloon, the family we had seen making willow lawn furniture was holding a street meeting.

By the time I reached the meeting they were surrounded with spectators, all of them friends and acquaintances of mine. The family stopped singing soon after my arrival and the mother and the two older children gave their testimonies, after which the father preached a brief sermon on salvation. He invited anyone who wished to accept Jesus to come forward and they would pray with him. I was under such conviction at that time that finding God meant more to me than what the world would think, including those spectators! I was the only one who accepted the invitation.

I went forward and knelt on both knees in that street, before all those spectators, prayed and asked Jesus to forgive all my sins and save my soul, and He did. The preacher also prayed for me. I have not had one second since that night until the present moment, some sixty-two years later, when I have been tempted to go back on God, to go back into the world. There is not security except in Him.

Being a city fireman, I was subject to an emergency call at any time; therefore, I tarried at the meeting no longer than was necessary to find God. As I started to leave, a young man rushed over to congratulate me and he invited me to join his church and Sunday School. Now I had known this young man for sixteen years as what I had considered to be a personal friend, but this was the first time I knew that he was a member of the church or Sunday School. This is an example of what had been my spiritual environment.

I went to bed that night with the personal satisfaction that I had obeyed God by repenting of all my sins and asking him to save my soul. It was the wisest and most gratifying decision of my life.

When I awoke the next morning I found myself in a new world. I was literally a new creature in Christ Jesus; old things had passed away; behold, all things had become new! (11Corinthians 5:17) I never was a liar or a thief and, while I had always had a hunger for spiritual truth, I had, nevertheless, become an awful blasphemer; but Jesus had now given me a new heart and had made me a new creature.

The instant I awoke I seemed to be impressed that everything that I beheld had been created for the glory and the worship of God. As I looked out and saw the trees waving in the breeze, I remarked to myself, "Even the trees are clapping their hands to the Lord!" I was reminded later how silly it was to say the trees were clapping their hands to the Lord—trees have no hands.

Later I read in Isaiah 55:12, which says, "For ye shall go out with joy, and be led forth with peace: the mountains and the hills shall break forth before you with singing, and all the trees of the field shall clap their hands." Also Psalm 96:12, "Let the field be joyful, and the trees therein: then shall all the trees rejoice."

My Spirit-filled brother had given me a little New Testament some fourteen months earlier, at a time when my desire for spiritual things was at its lowest ebb. Consequently, at that time, the Bible meant no more to me than Greek mythology or a fairy story, as far as understanding it was concerned. This morning, however, it was different, for it was like picking up something with life in it and almost every page I turned seemed to have a Scripture every newborn Christian should know. They stood out like signboards.

The divine revelation God gave to me that morning of the infallibility of the Holy Bible, as its being God's very own, divine, eternal Word to mortal man has been the greatest faith-stabilizing influence of my life.

The Lord had now given me, by divine inspiration, a knowledge of the importance of his divine, infallible Word and the necessity for consistent study of the Bible by those who wish to grow in grace, knowledge and wisdom, and to become fruitful Christians.

One of the most inspiring characteristics of the Bible, is that, regardless of how often we read it, we will always find Scriptures that will bless our souls and spirits, as though we had never read them before. This is one of the infallible proofs of the inexhaustibility of the Bible. I fell so in love with the Bible that I almost ate that little New Testament!

Now the Lord had another companion truth to the Bible with which I needed to become familiar, and that was the tremendous power of prayer. God's Word and prayer are so closely related that they form the basis upon which all fruitful Christian accomplishments are founded.

The Lord knew that I would be remaining in my hometown for the next fourteen months before moving to Dallas, and that I would have little if any, Christian fellowship during that period; therefore, He revealed to me through His Word the incomparable power of prayer (Matthew 17:21, "Howbeit this kind goeth not out but by prayer and fasting."), which, together with God's Word, sustained not only my spiritual equilibrium during that fourteen month period, but has been the guiding force in my entire spiritual and physical life since that time.

On my way to and from my home for meals, I had to pass the house where the minister and his family who had conducted the street meeting were living, and on the way back to the station from my breakfast that morning following my conversation, I met the minister in the middle of the street which we were both crossing in opposite directions, he coming from the market with meat for his family and I on my way back to the station from my home.

He seemed to recognize me some ten feet away. With tears in his eyes he extended me his hand and spoke the following words, "We saw visions in Waco the other night. The Lord said to go to Marlin and gather in his sheaves. The instant I saw you I recognized you as one of them." As far as I know I was his only convert; however, we never know what might eventually result from a seed-sowing effort such as this family put forth in Marlin."

During the early days of my born-again Christian experience I went through a very confusing period concerning the Holy Spirit. The minister in whose street meeting I was saved, without any preliminary explanation, said, "Now, Brother McMath, you know you cannot go to heaven without the Holy Spirit baptism." I now know this is not true, but didn't know it then.

Now I knew I was a born-again Christian because of the life-transforming experience I had received at conversion, and by the revelation the Lord had given me of his supernaturalness and the infallibility of His Word.

I knew I had to be saved before I could receive the Holy Spirit baptism, but now to tell me I could not go to heaven without the Spirit baptism was like nullifying the validity of my salvation. Consequently, it was not until I moved to Dallas in June 1917 and joined the only Pentecostal church in the city that I got the victory over my confusion and began seeking the Holy Spirit.

I went to the altar to seek the Holy Spirit one night soon after moving to Dallas. While praising the Lord with my hands raised I began laughing and continued for several minutes, after which I decided to see if I could stop, and I did. Now, while that was a pleasant experience, I did not then, and neither do I now, accept it as the baptism in the Holy Spirit.

I went back to the altar at the next church service again to pray for the Holy Spirit baptism. I no more than knelt at the altar when the pastor and his assistant both knelt, one on each side of me, and whispered in my ears, "Brother McMath, you received the Holy Spirit baptism the other night.

Now you refrain from seeking the Holy Spirit for yourself at the altar and begin praying for others to receive.

As was the belief in Pentecostal churches of this time, speaking in tongues was the initial evidence of being filled with the Holy Spirit. I was not aware at this time that the pastor had changed his belief or opinion that speaking in tongues was the initial evidence of the Holy Spirit baptism. I learned later that he was accepting people into the fellowship as Spirit-baptized saints who had never spoken in tongues. As a matter of fact, some fifteen months following this incident, the church was split over his liberal position favoring the Holy Ghost baptism without speaking in tongues. This issue is still controversial in churches today.

You can imagine how I felt after having just recovered from the statement by a minister that I could not go to heaven without the Holy Ghost baptism, and now being told I had received the Holy Spirit, when I knew that I had not. To add even more to my disappointment, I was asked not to seek the Holy Spirit any longer at the altar, but to pray for others to receive instead. This would have been good advice for a new genuine Spirit-baptized believer who spoke in tongues, but not for a Holy Spirit seeker.

Now the Lord no doubt took note of my plight after the ill advice and misinformation I had received from these different men, each of whom should have known better, culminating in my being asked to refrain from further praying at the altar for the Holy Spirit, with no other church or altar I could go to. Therefore, the Lord seemed to take me out of the hands of men and gave me the Holy Spirit in His own way, as follows:

Less than one month after this incident with the pastor I had a dream of oil being poured upon my head. Now you would ordinarily under such circumstances, expect at least some of such oil to run off. However, this oil typified the Spirit of God. Consequently every drop penetrated my being, as does the Holy Spirit when you are baptized with Him. Even though I did not understand what it was all about, nevertheless, because of its pleasant feeling, I had no objection, to pour until every fiber of my being was fully saturated with oil.

The instant the oil stopped pouring, a voice spoke to my heart and proclaimed, "This is the power of God!" and I raised my hands immediately and began praising the Lord Jesus with all my heart in English, the only language I knew. In a few seconds I began speaking in an unknown tongue just as fluently as I had ever heard anyone speak in an unknown tongue before or since.

This will conclude, at least for the time being, a brief account of some of God's dealings in my life over a period of sixteen years prior to my conversion in April 1916 and for a period of seventeen months following my conversion. To relate the many wonderful things God has done for me, and the many things He has helped me to do, would require a book. While I fully realize such a book would be of very little interest to any but relatives and close friends, I nevertheless hope some day to finish a book I have already started, as a gift to members of the family and friends.

Middle Car, 1st man is J.B. McMath, Fire Station, Marlin, Texas.

Picture taken in 1914
Driver - C.I. Fant
Left to Right Sitting
Good Boy Pierson
George Nunally
J.B. McMath
Vincent Marek
Standing - Paul Clements

J.B. McMath, with the reins

J.B. on street corner in Marlin, TX where he was saved

Minor Warren McMath.

Sign painted in 1912 by Minor McMath in Dallas, TX

Chapter Three:

J.B.'s Brother Dale and his World War 1 Experiences Including his Dream or Night Vision by J.B. McMath, Sr.

My family were living in the town of Marlin, Texas when my younger brother Dale (you probably remember him from his escapades in Galveston when he left the hotel room to wander on his own as a tiny boy) joined the Texas National Guard, on February 3, 1916, just fourteen months and three days before the United States entered the war on April 6, 1917. It was my candid belief and prediction that the United States would become involved in the war before it was over.

With this firm conviction I strenuously opposed Dale's joining the National Guard, realizing he would be mustered into the regular army immediately upon the declaration of war, and would be subject to overseas combat duty thereafter. Our Father, however, was finally persuaded to sign for him and he was sworn into the regular army, and did see duty overseas as was predicted. Records of dates of some of Dale's movements have been lost, therefore any events where actual dates are not given, are to be accepted, as memory will permit. Naturally, Dale, as well as his discharge papers have been consulted concerning dates and places.

The National Guard was ordered to Mercedes, Texas, for Texas Border Patrol duty (history has repeated itself here, hasn't it?) only a short while before our Father's death, which occurred on July the 7th, 1916. Therefore, Dale was on duty in Mercedes when notified of his death, and was unable to attend his funeral. The Guard went to San Antonio for a brief counseling with regular army officials, before proceeding to Mercedes. The order to Mercedes was occasioned by some of Poncho Villa's escapades along the Texas Mexican border.

The guard unit was eventually moved from Mercedes to Freeport to protect the sulphur mines there, and then to Corpus Christi for a brief stay before returning home to Marlin on April 3, 1917.

Dale had only been home 3 days when he was ordered on April 6th to return to Mercedes.

While a large crowd of citizens was gathered at the depot to see their soldiers off on their second expedition, the following Western Union Telegram from President Woodrow Wilson in Washington was read, "A state of war exists between the United States and Germany."

This very sudden change of events necessitated the changing of their plans from going to Mercedes. They went to San Antonio instead, for swearing into the regular army, by General John T. Pershing.

After the swearing in ceremony, they went to Corpus Christi where they stayed approximately three months before proceeding to Camp Bowie at Fort Worth, where they finished their training as well as their home stay, before going overseas. Dale's unit was assigned to the famous 26th division, 143rd Regiment, 72nd Brigade. Dale's army was No.1,496,236, and he was a bugler.

He was stationed at Camp Bowie in Fort Worth for approximately one year, before sailing on July 18, 1918 for overseas duty in France.

Coincidentally, every member of our family living in Marlin with the exception of myself moved to Dallas at about the same time Dale moved to Camp Bowie. The distance between Dallas and Camp Bowie was about 35 miles, and made it very convenient for the family to see Dale often during his 12 month stay there. As before mentioned Dale sailed for France on July 18th, 1918, and the war ended on his 22nd birthday November 11, 1918, just seven days short of five months from the day he sailed from American shores.

This was a birthday to always remember and thank God for.

His battle, engagements and expeditions according to his discharge papers were Muse-Argonne, Champagne, France.

His discharge papers also show that he was honorably discharged from the service of the United States on the 12th day of July 1919, by reason of demobilization. Naturally the United States had materials scattered over most of the allied war zone, and therefore many soldiers could not return home until all that material was gathered together and transported to a seaport for salvaging and shipping home.

Dale happened to be one of those chosen to help perform this task, and was therefore not able to sail home until June 30, 1919, some 6 months and 19 days after the Armistice was signed, and just 12 days before his discharge.

I am sure Dale could have given us accounts of many interesting experiences during his army life, some very amusing and others very sad and thought provoking. However, this very brief resume or history of Dale's army life was prompted primarily by what I sincerely believe to have been a God-given dream or vision which appeared to me after the war ended.

Therefore the foregoing is more or less a prelude or introduction to the account, which follows, and has to do with an experience I had soon after the war ended. Dale's joining the Armed Forces left me the only unmarried male member of the family who was old enough to help support our widowed mother, two teenaged sisters, and two 8 -year old twin brothers.

I registered for the draft on June 5th, 1917, and because of our dependents I was classified 3A, and when a review was made at a later date, I was retained in 3A, and remained there for the duration of the war.

As above stated the first general registration took place on June 5th, 1917, Dale was 20 years and five months old, and I was 22 years and 9 months old at the time. You will recall that I opposed Dales joining the National Guard, and if I had been successful in my opposition, I would no doubt have been drafted into the Army instead of Dale because of the differences in our ages, and he would have been exempted to help support the family, and according to my dream, I might have been killed.

Several months after the war had ended, I had a night vision in which I found myself in Germany, with the U.S. Army, and while walking along a railroad track, with no friend or acquaintance within miles of me that I knew of, I was suddenly confronted by three German soldiers who arose from a squatting position in some tall grass or foliage growing in the right of way where they had hidden.

The man standing in the middle was the largest and tallest of the three, and he had a rifle in his hands, and then he raised it to his shoulder and pointed it towards me.

Now I was some 5,000 miles from home, with no one I knew within miles of me, that I could say goodbye to, or that would hold my hand for a second before being ushered into eternity, I believe it was the most horrifying experience I have ever had.

And now the miracle happened, the very instant the soldiers gun reached firing position, a gun at my right, fired three times in rapid succession as an automatic pistol, and I turned instantly to my right to see who fired the gun, and it was my brother Dale, and I awoke.

There are four thoughts, which lead credence to the fact that the dream was of divine origin:

1. I sincerely believe Dale's gun saved my life.
2. There were three soldiers and three shots fired from Dale's gun.
3. The gun's deafening sound rang in my ear for several minutes after I awoke.
4. The gratitude and love for Dale that welled up in my heart.

Now, of course Dale had no thought that he may have saved my life by joining the National Guard, nevertheless the instant I awoke from my dream I was made to realize that Dale had in some manner saved my life, and the thought came instantly that it was his going to the war instead of me.

Naturally I loved Dale because he was my brother, and we were drawn somewhat closer together because of our nearness of ages. However, the love and appreciation for Dale, which seized my heart when I awoke that night from my horrifying experience, I believe, was supernatural and it has never left me.

Chapter 4

Dallas 1917

J.B.'s own words:

I moved to Dallas in early June 1917, and I had been in the city but a couple of weeks, when a young man from the church I was attending invited me to be the guest of a group of their young people at a jail service.

When we reached the Dallas County Jail I found another group from the same church already there awaiting us.

It was in this latter group that I met for the first time Miss Clara Mae Welch, 16 years and 9 months old, who became my bride 19 months later. We were introduced in late August of 1917. It embarrassed my wife for me to tell this story, for I usually start by saying I am going to tell you how I met my wife at a jail, and then allow as much time as possible to arouse curiosity and anxiety, before explaining what we were doing there.

Frankly I'm not so proud that I found her at a jail, but I am glad I found her somewhere. This was not the first time that I had been in love. I was desperately in love with a young lady while at the age of 22 years. This young lady was always willing to go with me anywhere I wanted to go but to church. Even though I did not think there was any other girl in the world that I would ever love I nevertheless made up my mind that I was going to serve God and that I could not afford to marry a girl that would not do likewise. Some time before Mae and I became interested in each other, she had become engaged to a young man of another faith. He attended her church with her regularly until they became engaged. He then told her they would go to his church after they married. She just slid her engagement ring off and put it in his coat pocket the first chance she got.

Clara Mae and I began seeing one another exclusively soon after that and on January 19, 1919, we were married by Reverend A.G. Garr at the old Fourth and Grand Tabernacle. We tried to get the minister to perform the ceremony before the evening service, but he insisted on waiting, and we found it was all a frame-up to allow people from another church to attend our wedding after their services, so we had a large crowd after all.

Now back to the rest of the jail story. There were about 12 of us in all, and one of the jail attendants escorted us by elevator to the top floor where it appeared the most hardened criminals were kept.

We stepped out into a bare vestibule or reception area and adjoining it was a large assembly cell for prisoners to assemble for various occasions.

Very soon a sizable group of prisoners were marched in and seated. In the group were these men who were condemned to death by hanging, the local method of execution in Texas at that time, now however, the electric chair is the legal method.

The meeting opened with a prayer, after which our leader sang several hymns followed by a number of personal testimonies and a brief sermon with the salvation message given.

After his message he asked if there were those who wished to accept Christ as Savior, and only one man stood up. He was one of the three men condemned to death. He stood and while weeping like a child says, "The Lord has saved my soul and has revealed to me in a dream that I am not going to be hung." The other two condemned men made no move at all and were both executed as scheduled.

Texas law forbids executing anyone for a capital crime committed while insane, and also forbids executing anyone who becomes insane after conviction.

Naturally the courts decide the facts of insanity.

If one is found to become insane after his conviction of a capital crime he is sent to an asylum for the criminally insane, and is supposed to remain there for life or until he regains his normal mentality at which time the death sentence is carried out unless perhaps he is pardoned. This prisoner was given a sanity hearing and judged insane. No doubt his own personal testimony at his hearing concerning his conversation and revelation from God that he wasn't going to be hung contributed greatly to what the court believed as sure evidence of his insanity. God is good because he used this to favor the criminal. He was sent to the asylum where he remained for several years and then he escaped.

About ten years after his escape, he was apprehended in the state of Tennessee and brought back to Dallas and re sentenced to death, this time in the electric chair.

I am sure some of you will recall Texas' only woman governor, Mrs. Miriam A. Ferguson, better known as "Ma" because of her initials. She happened to be governor at this time, and this mans case was brought to her attention in an appeal for mercy.

She made a personal investigation and found that he had married, was raising a family, was living as a law abiding citizen, and preaching the Gospel, so what did she do but give him an outright pardon. He is as free as I am today and is still preaching the Gospel.

Mae and J.B.

Letters

Prelude: Since J.B. McMath was a staunch businessman and a staunch Christian, little of his history revealed very much about his romantic relationship with his wife Clara Mae. Yet they did have a good marriage that lasted till death they did part from each other. The following letters written by J.B. and Clara Mae are included to give perspective on their day-to-day lives together, and how they felt about each other in more private settings.

New Orleans, Louisiana

January 19, 1927

Dear Precious sweetheart darling wife and children,

Dear, I was so glad to get your letter yesterday I hardly knew what to do.

The joyful thought of your coming down here was so exciting that I couldn't go to sleep, so you see I forgot finances and everything else and had to phone you so I could go to sleep.

But all the excitement and pep was gone when you said you would not come.

I guess people would think I was some baby if they knew how I was about home, but I don't ever want to get to where I will be satisfied away from home.

Well, I am sure you are using good judgment by not coming for it would cost so much money.

Mr. and Mrs. McBride took me for a drive Sunday afternoon. I sure did enjoy it.

I went to a Baptist Sunday School and church Sunday morning and had a very nice time.

Haven't seen Brother Jess since Saturday, but he was supposed to be here about three weeks.

Well, Shug, I see the men are putting the hoods on the signs so I guess they have come at last.

Now if the switch panels will come it won't be long before I can come home.

Tell J.B. Jr. that I miss him just as much as he does me I bet. I sure wish he were here with me.

Tell Rebecca Jane that I sure want to hear her cry or make any kind of noise for it would sound like music to me.

Well, dear sweetheart, I don't know anything to write more than I have already written, so will close for this time.

Kiss everyone in the house for me.

With everlasting love,

JBM

P.S. Answer immediately by special delivery only.

Dallas, Texas

January 19, 1927

Dearest sweetheart of mine,

I was so glad to hear your voice on the phone last night but couldn't understand half of what you said. I couldn't hear you, it was a bad connection.

Dear, you are so kind and thoughtful, after writing me yesterday, that you didn't feel able for me to take the jump, and then when you got my letter, you phoned I could come as you felt it would disappoint me if I couldn't.

Hon, I guess in the sweet by and by, you and I can take a trip and won't be bothered about finances.

Maybe we will have to wait though until Jesus comes for us.

But it will be a long, long vacation, and no expenses to worry us; our wonderful host will furnish every luxury free.

So this hope, refreshes our over taxed and tired and worn out bodies of the people all over the world who have faith in the second coming of Jesus.

Jesus says, "Be therefore patient unto the coming of the Lord."

Dear, I went over to see Sis Comp the other night, and in the bulletin it said A.G. Garr was to fill Sister McPherson's pulpit, while she is on her lecture tour. I am glad to know he is in line again. Also the McDowell sisters (the singers) wrote Sister Camp and said, "At last Dear Aimee is free, and on her way to preach the gospel, and we notice on her list (Dallas) and we know you people are glad." Brother Camp said New Orleans was listed too. (I left this in the letter because it is a reference to Aimee Simple McPherson, the noted woman evangelist)

How I wish you were here to go with me to see J.B.Jr. in his little play at school. I bought him a new pair of overalls to wear.

He is to wear a white shirt, and blue overalls.

Well, sweetheart, will say good by and come home just the minute you get through.

Bushels of love from all the babies and your wife,

Mae

New York, New York

Monday Night

April 1927

My Dearest Love,

Just a few lines to let you know how I am getting along, and what I am doing.

I got to Washington Sunday morning at 10:15 o'clock, and left there at 3:00 o'clock for New York so you can see I didn't have time to see very much, but I took two different sight seeing buses, one to see the city and one to see the suburbs. The city bus ride lasted one hour and the suburbs 2 hours and what I saw would fill a book. I saw Woodrow Wilson's home and the little porch where he made his last public address; this was also where he died.

We passed the church where President Coolidge worshipped and it was during church time and I was shown his big car parked in front of the church.

I also saw the theatre where Lincoln was shot and the room across the street where he died 9 hours later. They have an American flag hanging from the window of the room. I saw the home where Robert E. Lee lived for 35 years. Well, sweetheart, I saw so many things that it won't do to try to tell them all, but when I get home in the sweet by and by I will tell you everything. The only thing I have lacked having a perfect trip so far is you, you, you, my sweet precious darling.

Well, I got to New York last night a little past 8:00 o'clock and the hotel I went to was right in the center of the theatre district where all the electric signs are, so I walked down and I registered, then saw them.

I went to the Weinburgh office this morning and they seemed very glad to see me. Harold Weinburgh took me practically all over the business district today including the top of the Woolworth building.

You can know by how I am scratching this letter that I am in a hurry for Harold just brought me to the hotel a few minutes ago, and it is now 12:10 and I want to go to bed but I was determined to write you tonight.

Well sweetheart, I will stop and go to bed. Tell J.B. Jr. that I sure wish he could be up here with me and see this big old city for I know he would enjoy it much.

Kiss all 3 angels for me.

With lots of love and many kisses from your love,

JB

P.S. Don't forget to pray for me. I sure thank the Lord for helping me the way he has so far and am trusting him to continue so.

New York City, New York

April 14, 1927

Dearest Sweetheart and Angels,

Just another short letter to inform you of my movements.

I am still seeing New York and I never have been treated as well anywhere in my whole life as I have up here. Mr. Harold Wineburgh has taken me to every place of much interest that can be thought of.

I guess if nothing happens I will leave Saturday evening for Atlantic City, New Jersey, I will stay there Saturday night, and will go from there to Philadelphia. Sunday I will leave Philadelphia sometime for Chicago where I will spend Monday and maybe Monday night. From there I will go to Kansas City for at least one day and I guess home.

Well, sweetheart I sure do feel good up here for the weather has been fair every day since I got here, and it is cold enough for me to wear my coat everywhere I go.

Tell J.B. Jr. that I have something for him that I bought in New York. I won't tell him what it is until I get home so he can be anxiously waiting.

I am going to try and get some little something for all of you before I leave.

Well, sweetheart, I don't have anything more to write for I want to have lots to tell you when I get home. Please excuse this fast writing.

Sealed with a kiss for all of my jewels,

Your love,

JB

New York City

April 18, 1927

Dear Sweetheart,

I guess you are looking for me instead of a letter by this time.

But about the time I started to come home I got word that they were mailing some sketches from Dallas to New York for a big theatre sign which is to be bought in New York for Kansas City, so I have to stay here to figure them, and they are not here yet, so don't know just when I will leave.

You can rest assured that I am very anxious to leave for I sure do want to see you and my angels.

Well, sweetheart, I spent Sunday in Atlantic City, New Jersey, the famous city where they have the national bathing beauty contest each year. I will have lots to tell you about it when I get home.

Shug, if I had known I was going to be here as long as I have I sure would have had you to write me, but I didn't know and don't know yet, but I think I will be gone before you could answer this letter.

Well, sweetheart honeycomb, I have got to go eat supper and sure wish you were here to eat with me, but if nothing happens we will be eating together again by next Sunday I think.

Kiss all for me.

Your love,

JBM

Dallas, Texas

February 17, 1930

My Dearest Darling,

After attending church yesterday and spending the day with Nellie, and coming home to change Rebekah Jane's dress for evening service, I found your letters in the mailbox.

And how happy I am to know you had a safe trip, and that you have gotten your business started.

And work fast and don't let your little tootsies freeze off (ha, ha) and be sure to wear those wool socks.

Dear my Valentine verse was from your heart I know, and made me feel so good, that I wasn't quite so lonesome when I went to bed last night.

The children ask every day about you every morning, Rebekah Jane asks, "Where is Daddy?"

Darling, Brother Ridgeway asked me last night if you had a nice Sunday school attendance over at the Foursquare Church, as you were not at Bethel. I told him I thought that was a good one on you, and I was going to tell you and he sure laughed.

We had a sweet fellowship in the services and a very nice evening attendance.

Mr. Haas looked at our pecan trees and is going to prune them for $12.00. He said it was a shame that one was damaged so badly, you know the one in the front that Mr. Brown pruned.

Must bring this to a close, hoping to see you this week.

With bushels of love to my very own precious one, who is the only one in the world for me.

Lovingly,

Mae

Corpus Christi, Texas

August 8, 1934

Dearest Sweetheart,

We are enjoying our visit so much, and the drive down was made without any difficulties. We never made more than fifty miles an hour and our average was around forty or forty-five.

We went down in the Wonder Cave at San Marcos. Of course it couldn't be compared to Carlsbad, but to us it was a big thrill. We went down one hundred and twenty five feet deep underground. The guide said it had been an underground river that had made the different shaped rocks look like animals. It cost one dollar for admission.

I am making Sister Lawrence's home my stopping place. Brother Jessie and Sister Mrytle came by, also Velma and Merriman and Earleane and Dorothy and Alford who are with Sister Mrytle, and they all invited me to visit them. I ate supper with Mama and Papa last night and spent the night. Velma wants me to spend Monday with her, and Earleane Tuesday and Wednesday and Thursday with Brother Jessie and Sister Mrytle. They are going to take me fishing. I hope I catch a whopper.

Sister Florence and Mrytle and I went down to the beach yesterday. I went in bathing with Rebecca and Velma's little girl Phyllis Jean, and Sister Florence's little boy George.

Rebecca is just delighted with everything, but she said to me this morning she wished she could go home so she could see her daddy.

I am taking her every place I go, but leaving J.B. Jr. with Sister Florence, he and Billy are the same age and they are making the rounds together. I gave him the dollar you gave him.

Fanny said she didn't know what they were going to do about their trip, they had their car worked on but it still got hot and knocked.

And they are taking Marvin Elsworth with them on their trip so I suppose I had better bring their car back to Dallas, as there wouldn't be room in theirs for you.

I will leave Friday the 17th in order to be there the 18th as that is the day Willard starts his vacation.

Sister Florence said she wished you were here with us, she said when Mr. Stuart heard last year that we were in Galveston, he got insulted because we didn't come to Corpus, he asked Sister Florence if I could have gotten mad at her or gotten my feelings hurt.

I must say goodbye and God bless my sweetheart,

Mae

P.S. Please excuse my terrible handwriting

North Chicago, Illinois

January 19, 1946

Dearest Daddy,

I arrived safely at 9:45 p.m. Sunday night.

John met me at the train, and Rebecca had a nice meal waiting for me when we arrived. She had had it cooked since 8:00 o'clock.

My, my, that sure was a rough train that I rode on, and it was as slow as the Arkansas travelers train was back in pioneer times.

Dear, tell Dorothy Jo, I sat up real straight in my chair and every once in a while I would look over on my left shoulder and smell the sweet odor of the carnations and admire the beautiful red color of my corsage and would think of her and how sweet it was of her to give me such a nice gift to use on my trip.

Also, every once in a while I would open up my box of chocolates that Mr. Allen (Rebecca's father-in-law) gave me and would eat a luscious nut piece or cream one and think of how nice it was of him to give them to me. And when I would think of how kind and wonderful it was of you to make my trip possible by giving me my ticket, and making the many sacrifices of my personal waiting upon you during my absence. I was so happy with so many nice things to think about.

It sure was cold last night coming home from the station. Snow was everywhere.

It had fallen last week and had frozen over, John says another snow is predicted today. I am not going out in the fresh snow without overshoes.

Rebecca and John sure took a tumble in the snow. Rebecca's feet went out in front of her and she landed in a sitting position. John's feet went out also and he too landed in a sitting position. Another couple that were walking behind them also slipped and fell. So I think I am going to be real cautious walking upon new fallen snow. So dear maybe I had better caution you to be careful if it snows while you are here.

Oh, yes, Rebecca had another delicious chocolate pie baked and she said you missed out completely on it as she and I have already eaten it almost up.

John has a cold today and is running a little temperature, Rebecca has a cough, but Chippe is all o.k. and still is the center of attention.

Dear, I hope all has run smoothly concerning your business with connections and that you will be seeing us soon here in Chicago.

Lots of love, as ever, yours affectionately,

Mae

Friday morning

February 1, 1946

Dearest sweetheart,

As yet, I haven't received any word from you, as to your safe arrival.

But I am supposing you are back home, and also have had your trip to Memphis, Tennessee.

I do hope you were successful in buying the machine you wanted.

I made the trip back out to North Chicago, and upon arriving at the junction, I had to wait about five minutes for the street car, and it seemed that my legs were aching from the cold to the point that I couldn't hardly walk.

So when I got to the apartment I found out why, I was suffering so with my legs, it was 8 degrees below zero. But in about a couple of hours it turned warmer.

We have had it 8 degrees below zero again this Wednesday.

Also another snow has fallen since you left.

I sure will be glad when John and Rebecca (J.B. and Mae's daughter and son-in-law) Laura Lynn or John Junior whichever it will be, and myself start back to Texas, where it is so much more pleasant in the winter time, and where no soot is falling upon everything. We really have to keep busy cleaning all the time. We sent the curtains to be laundered, and I washed all the windows yesterday, so we can see out the windows a little bit better this morning.

We called on the couple that John and Rebecca associate with, and they remarked about you playing cards with them, they like you very much.

I imagine they found me rather dull; all I could do was listen to the radio, and look at the cute little boy of theirs.

They want us to come to dinner at their house next Sunday, but I don't know if we will go. Rebecca does not feel well enough to go any place or do anything; she hardly sleeps any at night. It seems her sinus trouble bothers her greatly, and with all her other aches and pains along with it, poor child. I am so glad I am with her so I can help her take care of John, Chipper (dog) and the apartment.

I do miss being with you, and do hope you are taking good care of yourself, and that everything is running along smoothly at the plant.

Dear, I started to church last Sunday morning, at the little Presbyterian Church then decided I would take a street car and try to locate an Assembly Church near North Chicago, possibly in Waukegan. So when I got to the street car in Waukegan, I stopped a driver and asked him to try and find a protestant church, so we drove to a Christian Church, but I told him that wasn't the one I wanted, that it would have to have the name Full Gospel, Foursquare, or Pentecostal on it. And he said, "Do you mean the church that believes in speaking in tongues?" And he said, "I don't know if there are any like that here in Waukegan or not but I do know that my brother went to one before he moved to Joliet, Illinois." But that church was in Zion, Illinois. And I asked him to take me there, and he said it would cost me $3.00 taxi fare. So he took me there and I arrived just as church started. I really did enjoy the services. It is a new church, and a fine congregation of people.

I met the pastor and wife, also the wife of a minister who worked with Brother Richie in Houston several years ago.

When I told him I was from Bethel Temple in Dallas they said, "Oh, we know of him, Brother Ott, also his son-in-law Jess Jackson, and Rex Jackson who traveled with Jess Jackson, and is now a missionary in a foreign field. This is his home church." They all seemed to think so much of both of the Jackson boys. I took the railway express back to North Chicago and got home by two o'clock.

Rebecca was beginning to wonder about me as I had told her the Presbyterian Church let out by 12 o'clock and I would be home a few minutes after that.

Well dear if you can send me some money the next time you write, as I want to feel free to do my part as I go along, and also buy me a few things I want for myself.

Also Rebecca's allotment arrives around the 2nd or 3rd day after the first of each month, so please send this to her when it arrives.

Lots of love to you,

Mae

North Chicago

February 11, 1946

Dearest sweetheart,

I received your most welcome letter last Friday morning.

I received also the money that was enclosed. Rebecca also received her allotment that you sent. We both have been looking around and doing a lot of shopping. There are lots of pretty clothes, but sizes are hard to find up here. I found a pretty suit at one store for $69.00. It was navy blue, and a white blouse and white gloves with it, and a black hat with patent pumps to match and a patent pocket book. It sure would have been good to buy all of them, so I could have made your eyes bulge out when you met me at the station, when I come home.

But as I didn't decide on the suit, I am still shopping around. There isn't any telling just what I will finally decide on. Maybe a bright suit, with red hat and red shoes and beige gloves and pocket book might make me look better, and make your eyes bulge out more. What do you suggest? Maybe you would prefer a dark green ensemble or maybe I had better take what I can get in my size the next time I decide to buy. And then it will depend on how much you send me next time you get flushed with green bucks.

Dear, I am so disgusted with Everets' bookkeeping; I am positive that statement was in error. Rebecca's account was clean months ago.

Please don't throw any of the receipts away that are in any of the drawers so when I come home I can straighten them out. And remember if they send us a statement saying we owe a balance just ignore it as I positively do not owe them a cent.

Dear, I had a good day yesterday. I attended Sunday school and church in Zion, Illinois and ate dinner with a lovely family named Hannithorpe originally from Switchlod. They took me to the famous Davis Church, which is called Christian Catholic Church. They have a choir of 100 voices. It is the church that Brother Bosworth attended when he was a very young man, and he played in their orchestra before he received light on the baptism of the Holy Spirit. It is as large as the Moody Church in Chicago. I sure received a blessing from their services. They have a passion play each year, with a cast of three hundred, and many hundreds are turned away each year because of not making accommodations in time. If I am here I expect to see it.

John's camp is closing down next month, and he may get to discharge then instead of May. Or he may be sent to his induction center near or in Dallas for the month of April. So it seems he will be getting out sooner than expected.

Miss Allen wrote that Gilbert is with Ellas in Galveston waiting for his release. They are so happy that he is back. Ms. Allen just can hardly wait it seems for John to join him also. So dear, if John is sent ahead of May, maybe you should get Chippe's fence fixed next month. I am sure she is looking forward to arriving at her Grandfather's back yard where she can chase cats away. I took her for a walk this evening on her leash, you should have seen her enjoy running over leaves and snow clods along the sidewalk.

We have just lovely weather one day, and just intolerable cold and snow the next.

Dear, I hope you are all o.k. I miss you a lot, and think of you every day and I also remember you in prayer.

Lots of love,

Your sweetheart,

Mae

Monday morning

Dearest Sweetheart,

Hope everything is all o.k. with you, Son, Mildred, and children,

Rebecca and I have really had a fine trip, no trouble in any way. We stopped and had the battery charged the morning we left. It was so cold and pleasant we just kept driving, and arrived in Chicago 8:30 a.m. the next morning.

We stayed at the Coolidge two days, and after almost giving up, finally found an apartment consisting of a large bedroom and separate cooking and eating room with an electric refrigerator, and at a reasonable price. We are still in West Chicago close to John's school.

Rebecca has gone every day and stayed a couple of hours with John while he was confined in sickbay. Dear, you should see how Rebecca gets around here. She can drive anyplace and anytime and keep her balance.

But I wouldn't dare to even attempt driving here not even to the market, which is only five blocks away. I feel I would get run over as everyone drives as if they were going to a fire! It is almost the same with the buses and streetcars. One has to run into one, and run out of one, or you will keep traveling with the throng.

Rebecca and I attended church Sunday morning at the Moody Church and we both enjoyed it very much, it surely is a great church. As Rebecca visited John Sunday night I returned Sunday night to church on the street car and since then I go any place I want to on the car and bus line, however, I haven't tried the subway or elevated yet. But think I will attempt it before leaving Chicago.

Tuesday morn

John came home with Rebecca and ate a chicken dinner (that Rebecca prepared all alone) and they went to the zoo, as he is free from fever now. He sure looks thin and he still has a cold or hay fever.

They sent most of the boys away to the Great Lakes Friday and next Friday I suppose John will leave with the last group.

He still isn't sure just where he will be placed. If he is sent to the Pacific he wants Rebecca to locate at his port in California, as he would get to come in ever so often.

And if she does go to California within the next ten days, what do you think about me remaining here to drive with her?

My only reason for not remaining is I wouldn't get to be with Son (J.B., Jr.) again until his next furlough and I sure would hate to do that.

On the other hand I feel Rebecca needs me along with her. Talk it over with Son and you let me know what you both think about it.

Dear, I wish you and J.B. and Mildred and Johnny and Gwendolyn (J. B. and Mae's son and wife and grandchildren) would drive to California and I could come back with you. If Rebecca has to go there, wouldn't that be grand?

Well, I must close now and you kiss little lambkins for Rebecca and I and lots of love to you, Mildred and J.B. Jr.

As ever your sweetheart,

Mae

June 26, 1950

Mexico City, Mexico

My Dearest Darling,

We arrived here in Mexico City safe and sound Saturday night, and were fortunate in getting accommodations at the Del Prado.

Now we are located here at Shirley Courts, and like it just fine, and it is so much cheaper too.

We are going about seeing sights, and learning to bargain for things we want. We are told that no one expects you to buy at the first price quoted but they come down every time.

When we started to the bullfight yesterday and we got into the cab we got our price first before letting them take us out because they will raise the price when you get there so they work both ways. Onleane and I attended church yesterday at a Union Evangelical English speaking church and met a girl there who knows Mildred real well. She and her husband have lived here six years.

Dear, I miss you not being with me and trust you are missing me. I hope you are doing fine without me though.

Mexico City is a very interesting place, and is just simply beautiful beyond words to describe, with beauty of color.

But they are suffering for lack of rains as their water supply is short, and tourists are asked to cooperate.

We plan on going down to Taxco for a couple of days, but have decided to omit Talcupa, as all tourists are disappointed there.

Dear, call Mildred and tell her about Mrs. Callaway, she was Minnie Blalock before marrying. She was a Bonham girl. Her brother Jack Bailey Blalock was also a close friend of Raymond's (Mildred's brother).

So far we are all well. I had a little sick spell coming down, but Shirley Coasts furnished food for airlines and it was good. So glad D's Addison recommended it. Lots of love to you.

Your sweetheart,

Mae

Tuesday 29th

Dearest sweetheart,

We are driving down this evening to Taxco, which is about a half days drive, and spending two days. They say Taxco is so typical of the native life and also where the silver mines are and where all the jewelry is made.

Dear, it is now the rainy season, it rains every day around 7 o'clock at evening for about a half hour and no one minds it. It seems things go on, as they should.

Love,

I sure miss you

Mae

Sunday evening

July 1, 1950

Dearest Sweetheart,

We have returned from Taxco and other points of interest, and now lock in our plans here at Shirley's.

We attended church here this morning and this afternoon drove out to the floating gardens and rode in a canoe down the river, and each of us bought an orchid, for only 2 pesos, which is less than a dollar in our American money.

Well dear, I guess we will be heading back towards the states soon. Glo said Tuesday we would start back so we should be at the border by Saturday. We may drive by to say hello to Sam and Edna (J.B.'s brother and sister-in-law) in Del Rio. Expect to see you just as soon as I can, I have had a most wonderful trip; it has been so enlightening and so new and different to our way of life.

However, the good old U.S.A. is a wonderful place to live, and the English language sounds wonderful to me.

We attended a grand opera last night and it was all in Italian.

It will sure be nice to see you again, and it feels like it has been ages since I left Dallas and you.

Hope all is o.k. with you.

Lots of love, yours always, Your sweetheart,

Mae

Rebecca Allen and Mae Mcmath

Chapter 5

The history of Neon Signs in the State of Texas

Prelude: This article written in the 1980's tells the history of the neon sign business in Texas from its beginning until the 1980's. This particular manuscript was an original typed manuscript but did not have J.B. Sr.'s authorship on it. From reading it, I have to assume he wrote it because it was so favorable and complete about him and his accomplishments. .

I feel I must also include this quote from the movie The Graduate from the 1960's because that is what this chapter's growth in plastics reminds me of. In the film Dustin Hoffman plays a young man who has just graduated from college. His father throws him a graduation party, in which he is not very excited about attending. During the party each of his father's friends give him advice about his future. One friend says, "I just have one word for you, Ben. That's plastics. Think about it." When I began to read this article it reminded me of the quote and I think you will catch the inference, History does have a way of repeating itself.

We are living in a time that future historians know best as The Golden Age of Commercial Exuberance! These days we only have to look down the street to view the evidence of an ever expanding commercial environment; skyscrapers surround us, franchises abound us, and there are far more distractions than a person needs in a lifetime. The options for governing our daily lives are so numerous now that the smallest decision can become a deliberation. The telephone book has become our most accessible reference to the gigantic commercial world around us. But perhaps even more indicative of our commercial evolution, and certainly more prominent in our history than a telephone book, is the ever-present outdoor advertising sign.

Signs have always served for one primary reason—to communicate information. As long as we have the basic desire to communicate, signs will always be an important element in our society. On various levels advertising signs do more than just persuade or command us, they record our history. Putting a sense of "image" in our lives, signs uniquely reflect changing lifestyles. The Sign Industry's national trade magazine beautifully sums up this concept in its very title, "Signs of the Times."

There is an intricate association that can be drawn between new commercial (and social) trends of our society and the advertising signs that are spawned by the trends. Trends are man-made phenomena. So are signs. Both are constantly changing, creating with contemporary modernism in mind. On one hand, trends are created in response to a changing environment, limited only by man's ideology. Trends are constantly affected by new technological achievements, with new technology comes a new trend of events. On the other hand, advertising signs reflect changing popular trends in a society, limited only in design by contemporary technology. Signs are constantly affected by the new ideology brought about with trends. Every new variation on an old theme brings with it a new design, a new image that must be communicated to society.

This discussion should rightfully lead to a serious sociological dissertation, but I am not a sociologist and this exordium is no place for that anyway. I am a preservationist, and the main point I want to bring to public attention is that through time advertising signs have been, are, and will always be intimately involved in the processes of commercial (and social) evolution. No industry has ever reached more people, affected more people and represented more people than the Outdoor Advertising Industry. For the moment, let us set aside the topical criticism that outdoor advertising creates an aesthetically unpleasant "visual clutter," and instead let us step back objectively to examine our society, and us and determine whether the Outdoor Advertising Industry is accurately producing "signs of the times."

We are more than a century removed from the early days of the "wall dogs," "barn stormers" and drifters who made their living painting signs on the expansive walls of new commercial buildings and barns. We are an era removed from the vanishing silver and gold leaf men who took pride in embellishing office windows and doors with their signs. We are past the development period of electrically illuminated signs in America, and we are past the 'neon' period of sign making—which characterized our rapid commercial growth in the 20th century. The current trend in outdoor advertising should be obvious by now; it is practically thirty years old already.

We have progressed rapidly in the production of vacuum-formed plastic advertising signs since the 1950's. Similar to all previous trends in sign production, plastic signs were introduced to satisfy a desire for more modern looking signs. However, unlike previous trends in outdoor advertising, plastic sign production was born in America out of the necessity for a sign that could be mass produced and safely shipped throughout the world. This marks a significant era in our commercial history. As never before Americans now have the opportunity to establish their economic 'image' in national and international proportions. The new mass produced plastic signs make this large-scale image-making process possible.

Naturally, future trends are constantly speculated, but never actually defined until they are proven popular. Given the numerous and flexible applications of plastics in sign productions, plus the widespread infiltration of plastics into every possible market leads this author to believe that, in one form or another, plastics will remain with the Outdoor Advertising Industry for quite sometime in the future. Also, there are strong indications that the highly expensive and sophisticated electronic "time and temperature" signs will lead the next trend in outdoor advertising. As the current rate of technological progress it would even be conceivable to predict we will see our first three-dimensional laser beam sign in the near future.

The development of neon tube lighting, like most outstanding developments of the current age, can be attributed to a long history of worldwide research and invention culminating in the origin of a tremendous growth and total saturation of the neon sign industry. The origin of gaseous tube lighting can be traced back to the late 17th century when it was observed that a faint light was produced after shaking a simple vacuum tube filled with mercury. Pioneer research in this field of electric-luminescence was conducted by a German physicist named Geissler in the 1850's, who invented the first practical prototype of the modern electric discharge (neon) tube. Further experiments by Geissler and others yielded the fundamental theory that all gases will conduct an electric current, and thereby produce light, and that certain inert gases (discovered in 1894) will glow in characteristic colors when bombarded with high voltage current.

Although only the common gases, nitrogen and carbon dioxide were used in the initial laboratory experiments, two Englishmen, Sir William Ramsey and M.W. Travers made a notable achievement in 1898. In the process of isolating the inert gases, argon and helium, they discovered three rare gases; xenon, krypton, and neon, meaning "the new one," is present in the atmosphere at a rate of approximately one part in every 16,000 parts, and it is characterized by its unusually high electrical conductivity and its brilliant red-orange glow. Despite the fact that Ramsey and Travers' process for isolating the rare gases was not economically feasible for large-scale rarefication, neon was still regarded as a promising source of illumination for the 20th century. Had it not been for the continued research of a French scientist-inventor named George Claude, the early neon glow tubes would have remained a mere laboratory curiosity.

Claude is widely recognized as the father of the neon sign industry because of his significant contributions toward commercializing the various components of gaseous tubes. During the early years of the present century he had perfected the means for obtaining inexpensive, industrial quantities of the rare gases through fractional distillation of air. Furthermore, Claude had discovered that the life of a glow tube depends primarily on the endurance of the electrodes that are sealed to both ends of the tube. Consequently, he developed and patented the first high resistance, non-corrosive electrode, and from that point onward the evolution of neon gas signs were rapid.

Since the earliest days of electric sign lighting there was a demand for a low consumption lamp with long burning life, but not until the emergence of Claude's neon tubes in 1910 were the requirements for such lamps satisfactorily met. The illumination produced by rarefied gases was not wholly suitable for interior lighting because of its deficiency in certain wavelengths of light, but the novel effects that could be achieved with bent gas filled tubes was totally adaptable to outdoor advertising. With the formation of the Claude Neon Lights Company of France, the first commercial neon signs began appearing in Paris in 1910. Within a decade the neon sign industry was born.

Realizing the commercial success of neon signs, Claude proceeded to expand his potential market by selling franchise licenses to other countries. In 1924 the first American neon plant was established in New York, and in a few years sales representatives for Claude Neon proliferated throughout the east and west coasts of the United States. America was particularly receptive to the introduction of neon advertising in the 1920's. The inherent colors and vibrancy of the new medium epitomized the very essence of renewed commercial vitality that the country was experiencing during that decade. Owing to aggressive neon salesman working eastward from Los Angeles and westward from New York, it is no wonder that America's new self-proclaimed image was affected in every state prior to the depression of 1929. It was in this manner that neon signs were introduced to the Texas market in 1926, only two short years after the first neon plant was established in this country.

The purpose of this work is to establish a record of the "neon" years of commercial sign making in Texas; roughly 1926 to 1955. This is the period that is recognized as the rise and fall of neon sign production in Texas, with peak years occurring after World War II. Although this is an in-depth study of Texas neon sign production, it is also indicative of neon production around the United States during the same period, and the dates sighted in this history can be used to approximate general trends in it's development throughout the country. Therefore, the underlying significance of this documentation transcends mere geographic boundaries.

The heyday of neon sign making is over. It was a colorful and intriguing period in electric-sign history that literally illuminated the way for our 20th century commercial expansion. This is not to imply that the techniques of manufacturing neon signs are extinct—quite the opposite. There are still many independent sign men who do nothing but manufacture and repair neon signs. In fact, some authorities will insist that there is more linear feet of neon produced today than ever before. But in harsh contrast with the spectacular neon displays of the 1930's and 1940's neon in the 1980's has diminished to a subordinate role in outdoor advertising; serving primarily as a hidden light source for the popular plastic and metal channel letter signs. Indeed, the artistry is gone, and the pride and gratification of creating artistic neon spectaculars is just a memory for countless, old time neon sign practitioners.

Texas is the home of numerous, distinguished old timers in the Outdoor Advertising Industry who were instrumental in initiating and propelling the neon trend in the state. They are the glass blowers, the sheet metal men, the electricians, designers, salesmen, and sign painters whose glorious careers in the neon sign business compromise its very history. These are the individuals that I sought to accurately recount the history of neon sign making in Texas. Regretfully, many of the original neon pioneers in the state are deceased, but their lifelong accomplishments have endured in the memories of their survivors and in the scrapbooks that were kept over the years. The black and white photographs that appear in this text are reproduced with permission from the prominent sign men who kept such scrapbooks.

Finally, I have been told frequently during the course of this work that I am about ten or fifteen years too late to be photographing neon signs. Many of the best old spectaculars that were made during the heyday of neon signs have long been salvaged or scrapped. Fortunately, some neon signs have outlived the heyday and classic vestiges can still be seen lighting the Texas night. After focusing on hundreds of neon signs the photographs I have chosen to include in this article represent a broad cross-section of styles, applications, and history of neon sign making in Texas.

The 1920's was, indeed, a roaring decade for Texas business. Never before was the consumer market so motivating for the influx of new commodities, services, and specialized trades. With the advent of mass production techniques the major Texas cities began sprawling with multi-story factories and stores to accommodate the needs of their growing populations. As early suburban settlement was taking place the ubiquitous Main Street was still the only place to go for mainstream activities of the time. The central business district was a city's vital source of work, recreation, education and commerce and in every downtown there were commercial sign painters to direct traffic.

Texas sign makers were enjoying the business from a growing and prosperous commercial environment in the 1920's. Advertising signs were in big demand, and the wages for a competent sign worker were above average for the time. It is interesting to note that as 20th century business was thriving in an atmosphere of high volume and mass production, the commercial sign painters were utilizing handcrafted methods established over a half-century earlier. There was no machine that could replace the artistry of a diverse sign man. Yet, as more people were discovering the multitudinous nocturnal diversions that downtown had to offer the advertisers became concerned that their Gold Leaf, Black Smaltz, and hand painted signs, however beautiful by day, were not so effective at night.

The very earliest illuminated signs used gooseneck floodlights to light ordinary hand painted signs, but for most applications that was not enough. The first commercial signs that appeared in Texas in the 1920's were usually made and sold by Federal Electric of Flex-Lume Electrical Advertising Company, with home bases in Chicago and New York respectively. These were called "Opalite" signs, and a variety of businesses used them. They consisted of simple incandescent fixtures situated in a square wooden frame and concealed behind a piece of frosted, opal glass on which the advertisement was painted. Various patents were granted for the internal reflecting device, but the effect of silhouetted letters was basically the same. It is recalled that the early Opalite signs appearing in Austin during this time were 'V' shaped, employing frosted glass on two sides, and were generally hung under the awning of the store. Abilene boasts one of the original electric signs distributed by General Motors in the 1920's. These were large sheet metal signs with cut-outs for inserting individual letters made of opal glass, also illuminated from inside.

However as exciting as those first Opalite signs were, they were not necessarily the electric signs that bedazzled the decade. The spectacular electric signs (that were veritable credits to their city) were purchased primarily by major theatres, hotels, and better department stores. They were large metal signs with vast arrays of incandescent bulbs, Colors were obtained by placing translucent colored hoods over individual bulbs. Many theatres, most notably the Majestic and Texas Theatre chains, incorporated sophisticated mechanical flasher units to further enhance their signs. Prominent hotels such as the Herring in Amarillo and the Texas in Ft. Worth gained landmark status when their huge rooftop signs were erected high above the city.

Of considerable grandeur and notoriety was the early electrical display installed for Joske's Department Store in San Antonio. This sign actually pre-dated many of the bulb spectaculars associated with the 1920's, being erected on the roof of their main store in 1917. The sign, which read "JOSKE'S – THE BIG STORE", measured fifty square feet, weighed six tons, and was regarded as "the world's greatest electric sign".

"…Incandescent lights operated by a seven foot flasher showed a cowboy galloping after a running steer…the cowboy throws his lasso over his head to rope the steer…the steer was reared on its haunches and jerked on its back…then the sign went dark for a moment and the action was repeated. Meanwhile, an eight foot Texas star radiated alternate blue/green colors with the border flashing and whirling circles…changing colors… changing colors at each reversal."

Federal and Flex-Lume were the two major suppliers of electric signs and sign products in the beginning, but without the initiative of certain Texas sign manufacturers the large spectaculars would have been impossible to erect and maintain within the state. Outstanding in the history of Texas sign production is a Dallas-based company known as Texlite. Founded in 1879 by Italian immigrant F.S. Borich, an unassuming commercial sign shop evolved into one of the leading producers of electric bulb signs, and later neon signs, for the state and the entire country. As early as 1923 Borich Sign Company began manufacturing electric signs and the name was changed to Texlite Electric Sign Company. Six years later, under the ownership of a New Yorker named Harry Wineburgh, Texlite opened their first branch office in Atlanta, Georgia and was actively shipping electric signs to many states. One notable achievement that was made at the Dallas plant in 1927 was the electric spectacular for the Saenger Theatre in New Orleans. Purchased for $16,350.00, the sign loomed sixty-three feet high with 5,000 light bulbs. In fact, this was so huge (even by today's standards) that the front wall of the production facility had to be removed in order to get the sign out.

As these electric spectaculars were not cheap to make, or to operate, their prevalence clearly reflected the prosperity and orientation of the economy in the 1920's. The theater signs were some of the most ambitious projects undertaken by sign companies. They were state-of-the-art examples of what could be achieved with the combination of light, color, and motion, and virtually every night in Texas was alive with kinetic excitement. While most Texas sign manufacturers were reveling in the success of their new found electric expression, there were a few individuals who became aware of a completely and novel form of electric advertising—that being 'neon'. Little did they know, however, that neon would revolutionize their entire industry in years to come.

In 1926 neon signs first appeared in three cities of Texas almost simultaneously, but as a result of entirely different circumstances. East and west coast sign companies had marketed George Claude's patents for nearly two years and their sales representatives were scouring the rest of the country for potential neon customers. The broad geography of Texas was conveniently split between three primary Claude Neon franchises; the Denver, Los Angeles, and Chicago plants. There was enough business between them to prevent serious competition. Claude Neon in Denver took control of the Panhandle region by sending the earliest salesman with neon samples into Amarillo. Claude Neon Federal, a branch of Federal Electric in Chicago, had vigorous sales in Dallas, and later in Houston. Claude Neon representatives from Los Angeles were reported to have been the first suppliers of neon signs in San Antonio.

Usually these neon salesmen would come to town and approach a few prominent, local sign men until they found a willing party to act as sub-contractor for all subsequent sign erection and maintenance. Well known in south Texas, veteran sign maker George Bragg relates his initial experience of neon in 1926:

…About eight o'clock in the morning there…a big Cadillac pulled up in front (of my sign shop in San Antonio)…and two guys came in…They had a sample and it was the letter 'R' in red neon…They came in from California… there was no neon company here…that was one of these George Claude set-ups…Of course, when you see something like that (that) you never saw before in you life…well, it was really something!...So, I talked with them for a while, I said, "Let's sit down and see what a sign would cost"… The simplest thing is a café sign, six foot long with letters in red neon…so; we figured this sign up…just the word 'CAFÉ' was (pause) $650.00…! That's about $6000.00 today…!! I said, "Man, that's the most beautiful thing in the world, but you're never going to sell it"…I never saw them anymore…

As the story goes, Mr. Bragg turned the offer down, but his close friend in the bulletin sign business, James Ryan took the initiative and ordered two signs from these salesmen; one for Sommer's Drug Store and the other for Milam Cafeteria. In the 1930's, Ryan went on to create one of the leading neon sign companies in the southwest, Texas Neon Advertising Company in San Antonio.

Amid extravagant electric bulb signs already in operation, the first neon signs were somewhat overwhelming. They were no frill signs, rarely larger than 3 by 6 feet, with simple block letters in red neon tubing either affixed to a skeleton grid for hanging in windows, or as relief topography on a painted metal surface, but people would drive for miles just to stand and stare at a small, glowing neon sign; something akin to staring at the first television transmissions from the moon. The early users of neon signs were leased by the franchise manufacturers rather than sold outright to the advertisers. However, Mr. Bragg's initial skepticism was not uncommon, nor unfounded. There were complications with the first neon signs in Texas.

The typical contrast between Claude Neon franchises and their Texas subcontractors called for the glass tubing to be made to order, out of state, and shipped to Texas where it was assembled, installed, and maintained by local sign companies. In return, the Texas companies received a commission on all leases. Often, an electric technician from the home plant was transferred to Texas to instruct and supervise the assemblage and operation of neon signs. Nevertheless, the major state wide complication with this arrangement was that there was no guarantee the glass units would survive in one piece, and more often than not—the glass arrived broken. This was disconcerting to Texas sign men who were trying to promote neon sales in their cities, and the fact that there were no authorized Claude Neon franchises established in Texas until 1933 (when Federal set up their Arlington branch) was probably the reason why neon did not flourish as early as it did in New York or Los Angeles.

It was obvious from the beginning that if Texas was going to flow with the neon trend already established on the east and west coasts, it was essential that all phases of neon sign production had to be conducted in the state, thus avoiding any unnecessary time and transportation obstacles. Two events enabled this to happen. First, toward the end of the decade numerous neon supply houses had sprung up in the eastern cities making the components of a neon plant readily available throughout the country. Second, branched off into neon tube and electrode manufacturing, the QRS Devry Corporation, branched off into neon tube and electrode manufacturing. The QRS electrode was, at first, inferior to Claude's patented electrode, but it posed a serious threat to the Claude Empire because, unlike the Claude electrode, QRS was available to everyone. Later QRS and VOLT ARC would monopolize the market on electrodes.

Acquiring the hardware and setting up a neon plant was just one step toward demystifying the total neon process that was controlled for so long by the Claude patents and franchises. Neon production requires the specialized skills of a glass blower, pumper, and bombarder, not to mention the added intricacies involved in designing the neon signs at the drawing board. These were skills that few, if any, Texas sign men had at the outset. Texas' oldest neon pioneers learned the trade from men like Charlie Gump, Ray Clark, Paul Pfeiffer, Bill Grovsner, and Willy Flashour. They were highly experienced apparatus glass blowers and neon specialists working around New York and Chicago when neon was introduced there. In the 1920's they were circulating through Texas, helping various sign makers set up their own neon facilities, and teaching them the rudiments of neon sign making.

By 1929 Texas had begun to see the light of her own production. With at least five neon plants in operation around the state, the focus on electric advertising was definitely turning from incandescent to neon production. The first Texas cities that had their own neon plants were Amarillo, Ft. Worth, Dallas, San Antonio, and Houston. Whereas the actual history at this point is complicated with numerous accounts of "the first neon shops" in each city (that for some reason did not succeed and were absorbed by their competition), suffice it to say that the five instigative neon companies in 1929 were: HOAREL STONE, I.F. Hoarel-owner (Amarillo): CORN SIGNS, J. Corn-owner (Ft. Worth); TEXLITE, H. H. Wineburgh-owner, J.B. McMath-general manager (Dallas): TEXAS NEON ADVERTISING COMPANY, J. Ryan, W. Johnston-owners (San Antonio): and DIXIE NEON SIGN COMPANY, A.C. Bering-manager (Houston).

The 1930's was a significant decade for the expansion of the neon sign industry in Texas, a period when the ingenuity and ambition of sign men were unrestrained. The crews that originally consisted of east coast technicians were replaced by Texans newly trained in neon production; G.M. Jones, Jack Dempsey, George Bragg, Dick Mitchell, Frank Haden, H.K. Graham, Carl and George Houser are just a few of the widely recognized pioneer Texas glass blowers. In addition to the aforementioned companies, new competition was created within the state, and some older commercial sign shops began to establish their reputations in the neon fields. Notably, General Neon in San Antonio, City Sign Service in Amarillo, Matteson Outdoor Advertising in Houston, and Zimmerman and Sons in Dallas gained prominence early in the decade. As the number of neon plants multiplied and productivity increased, neon supply houses were started in Texas. In 1931, Charlie Reece formed his nationally known Reece Supply Company in Dallas with the backing of a Mr. Warren, and authority at the Claude Neon Federal plant in Chicago. Later, Texas Supply and Southwest Supply in Dallas, and Dallas Neon Supply in San Antonio were formed.

Texas was rapidly becoming the self-sufficient 'neon' state that resident sign makers had envisioned. In the early 1930's an important intra state market was developing from the incentive of a few sign men: Louis Hoarel, J.B. McMath, and Jack Corn among others. In Amarillo, Hoarel was operating one of the first neon plants in Texas, set up by a QRS representative in 1926. Although Hoarel had established his reputation on his excellent show card and lobby display work for the Fair Theatre (in Amarillo), he was enthusiastic about neon from the very beginning. As a licensed QRS representative in Texas, Hoarel set up his Western Neon Wholesale in the basement of his commercial sign shop in 1930. In much the same way that Claude Neon from Denver was operating a few years earlier, Hoarel was actively making his own neon signs to lease throughout the Panhandle. In this way, Hoarel introduced neon to many other cities in Texas by mid decade. He supplied the glasswork for some of the earliest neon signs in Lubbock, Abilene, Wichita Falls, and the Odessa-Midland community. By 1939, Hoarel had set up a branch plant in Hobbs, New Mexico and had also bought out R.L. Tessler's Hi-Glow Neon Sign Company, the pioneer neon company in Clovis, New Mexico. Within a decade after the first neon plant Hoarel Neon Sign Company had become "one of the largest neon sign manufacturers and distributors in the Southwest."

Meanwhile, in Dallas, J.B. McMath was supervising the installation of Texlite's first porcelain enamel furnace in 1930. Mr. Mac. as he is affectionately known, was the early construction foreman for the Borich Signs, and then the well respected plant superintendent and executive for Texlite Electric Sign Company. At that time he was probably supervising the largest crew of sign men in Texas, maintaining the reputation of high quality workmanship that he created for Texlite in the mid-1920's. Quality was an inherent feature in Texlite's first porcelain enamel neon signs, and they were sold throughout the state. With sales representatives assigned in Abilene, Austin, Corpus Christi, Houston, and San Antonio, Texlite porcelain was also rivaling the best in Houston and San Antonio; Texlite porcelain was rivaling the best that Federal in Chicago had to offer. When their second porcelain furnace was installed in 1937, it was allegedly the largest box type furnace in the world. It is recalled that Texlite gained wide recognition for the Saenger Theatre sign in 1927, but that was just a foreshadow of the spectacular porcelain and neon theatre fronts that they would become nationally famous for after WWII.

Of course, there are many other companies and events that reflected the growth of Texas' intra state neon sign market but the contributions of Jack Corn in the 1930's are worthy of mention. The same New York technicians who were hired by Texlite to teach neon sign making in Dallas immediately went to Corn Signs in Ft. Worth to do likewise. Corn's salesman covered a broad region in Texas between Wichita Falls in the north and Corsicana in the south, and by mid decade they had established a strong clientele of repeat customers. Corn featured signs of all sizes, but were notably responsible for some of the larger, more spectacular signs of the times. While Corn was supplying the tubing for the landmark Kemp and Holt Hotels in Wichita Falls, they were building "the largest neon sign in the southwest" commemorating the Ft. Worth Frontier Centennial. Facing the Centennial fairgrounds in Dallas, this enormous spectacular sign was 130 feet long, fifty feet high, and had twenty-four different flashing actions. Prior to these signs Corn takes credit for another remarkable sign appearing in Austin in 1932. Austin's Chamber of Commerce had asked the most prominent sign company in town Duplex Outdoor Advertising Company, to make a special neon sign for the Roosevelt election campaign that would be coming to the state capital. There were no neon plants in Austin at that time, as Texlite was supplying the majority of the city's neon. So, Duplex designed a spectacular sign for which Corn Signs made the tubing and supports. This sign was approximately 4 by 60 feet with rose red neon that read, "PROSPERITY'S ROSE BLOOMS AGAIN WITH ROOSEVELT".

Austin was a major city that did not feel the pressure to jump right into the early neon trend sweeping the state. After the city's first neon plant was set up in 1936, practically all of the signs produced there were for the local market. Austin has always been a commercial sign painter's town, and Duplex Outdoor Advertising Company has been the leading, innovative sign company there for over fifty-five years. Under the combined partnership of R.V. Miller, Arthur Baird, and later Ed St. John, Duplex was the first company in the state to develop the double-sided highway bulletin board. In 1926, they were employing a U.T. student as a part time show card artist. His name was Israel Tearlisky, a.k.a. Pat Tearle. After graduating Tearle went to Florida to manage a sign company, and he learned glass blowing and neon production there. He maintained a correspondence with St. John the whole time, and when he decided to move back to Texas around 1935, Duplex offered him a job. Tearle brought his knowledge of neon back to Austin, set up the first neon plant at Duplex, and taught Austin sign men the process. Tearle stayed with Duplex for four or five years before getting out of the sign business altogether, but during his career as a sign man he designed and made the glass for many signs that are still in use some forty five years later. The Alamo Hotel was a landmark job for Tearle. It is a rare example of neon signs made with Uranium Green tubing, a type of amber/green colored glass, containing uranium, that was only available for a short time mid to late 1930's (it was discontinued because of its discovered radioactivity). Another Tearle job; Joe Koen & Sons Jewelers was the first sign in Austin using "ruby red" tubing, a once common hard lead glass that is now expensive and hard to find.

Duplex gained national notoriety with another first in the state: spectacular outdoor bulletins embellished with neon. Their achievements were heralded in a "Signs of the Times" article in May 1945. "...Just before the war Duplex progress was celebrated with the unveiling of Austin's largest spectacular, The Gulf Brewing Company's Prize Beer Display, featuring the "Blue Match Man"...This spectacular sign was the largest of many attractive displays that had been designed and constructed in Austin in the company's plant and marked the beginning of a trend that will no doubt continue in that sector after the war... The prediction was correct." Neon-ized bulletins were popular advertising for the Pearl Brewing Company in San Antonio, Jax Beer in Galveston, and the Lubbock Foster Company made wide use of neon embellishment in the 1950's.

Neon sign makers have always prided themselves as craftsmen in a handcrafted industry. That fact remains true to this day. Neon signs are inherently one of a kind signs: designed, manufactured, and maintained according to the individual customer's order. In the neon sign industry, increased output does not necessarily mean cheaper production. Nevertheless, mass production is an invariable consequence in any industry when the demand for a product becomes as widespread as neon signs had become after Prohibition ended.

With the ratification of the 21st amendment on December 5, 1933, beer and liquor companies needed advertising signs in a big way. All across Texas wine and liquor stores literally sprung up overnight, and they, too, needed distinguishing signs. There is no doubt that the end of Prohibition was a great financial boon to the neon sign industry. In fact, sign makers had anticipated the extra business, and in some cases the added revenue from breweries and retail stores were realized even before alcohol was legal. What happened around 6th and Harrison streets, Amarillo's wet district in 1933, is a prime example. Louis Hoarel's right hand man in sign construction and election, M.M. "Fat" Crouch recalls the night of December 4, 1933 when wine and liquor stores, and their neon signs were still illegal. "…They wanted their signs hung up ahead of time so that whenever Prohibition ended, then they'd be ready to go…We put tow sacks over the signs before they were legal and tied it…and then at twelve o'clock that night (Dec. 5, 1933) well then, we'd pull the strings out and turn the signs on…"

Since 1934, the Texas law governing beer advertising has stated that no sign, advertising a particular brand, may be displayed on the exterior of a drinking establishment or retail store where that beer is sold. That spawned the development of the so-called "back bar" neon signs in the mid 1930's, and they are still being produced in extraordinary numbers today. They were small signs designed to be hung on any interior wall (within reach of an electrical outlet, of course), and usually behind the bar. With just the minimum of neon tubing and a small transformer tied on to a metal 'skeleton' grid, they were inexpensive signs to manufacture and very easy to maintain.

Evidence of early mass production techniques showed up in cities like Corpus Christi and San Antonio where beer companies contracted local sign men to manufacture large quantities of these signs to ship throughout the state. James Kirkpatrick, owner of Kirkpatrick Neon in Corpus Christi and San Antonio where beer companies contracted local sign men to manufacture large quantities of these signs to ship throughout the state. James Kirkpatrick, owner of Kirkpatrick Neon in Corpus Christi, was involved in this contract work in the 1930's. 'The topical question in those days', he recalls, 'was—"How many Schlitz can you make in a day?"' The neon tubing for back bar signs was still bended by hand, but wooden forms were often used to expedite the necessary bends, thus increasing total output. In San Antonio, George Bragg's main business for more than twenty-five years was making back bar signs (which were also popular with Metzger's and Borden's Dairies there in later years). His employees were trained to produce one complete sign every hour, thirty to forty each week, and the signs were sold to the distributor for an average of $22.50 each. That was a thoroughly lucrative business in the 1930's!

Up to the beginning of World War II the general feeling among Texas sign makers was that neon signs would likely continue to flourish forever. While oil and beer companies provided their bread and butter contracts, sign design and engineering experiments were developed for the local market. Despite the primitive block and tackle sign erection techniques that were still widely used before the war, every new spectacular sign that went up was bigger than the last. Perhaps the most outstanding, surviving reminder of ambitious sign engineering is the 'Flying Red Horse' in Dallas. It was J.B. McMath's crowning achievement for Texlite in 1934. Erected on the roof of the twenty-ninth story Magnolia Building (then the tallest in Dallas), the sign consists of two 30 by 40 foot porcelain enamel horses, joined in the middle by a system of metal struts, and festooned with 1200 feet of neon tubing. Furthermore, McMath designed it to revolve on a unique motorized platform controlled by a wind velocity thermostat. Six thousand pounds of bolts, struts, neon tubing, and porcelain panels were hauled to the top floor on an elevator, passed through a window, and hoisted up to the roof where it was assembled. The real engineering genius of the 'Flying Red Horse' is that every component was designed and made with such accuracy on the ground (before assembly) so it would all fit together perfectly on the roof of the Magnolia Building!

Indeed, it seemed like the neon sign business in the 1930's was a runaway industry in Texas, with many brilliant sign men and few restraints. But when World War II began, sign production suffered an all but deadly blow throughout the state. Beginning around 1940 it was becoming increasingly harder to sell neon signs. The bottom of the market had just about fallen out. As U.S. involvement in the war approached, sign materials were becoming scarce, and unless a sign man could scrounge supplies his production nearly stopped.

The proliferation of neon shops after the war can be attributed to numerous factors. First, there happened to be a number of second hand neon plants for sale by the companies that went broke during the blackouts. Many established commercial sign painters who had stayed out of neon production until this time took the opportunity to buy a cheap neon plant, and started making neon signs as a lucrative sideline. This is how two major companies: Modern Signs in Austin (Ralph Campbell, owner) and Pylant Sign Company in Midland (Thurman Pylant, owner) gained prominence in the neon sign market.

This is also the time when some ambitious, long-term employees of various neon companies split off to begin their own companies. For example, J.B. McMath, "the brains of Texlite", left Texlite in 1946 to form a partnership with Jack Axilrod as McAx Sign Company in Dallas. Jim Otterpohl, who had worked in sign construction and erection for three major San Antonio neon shops since 1931, joined his co- worker Clarence Simpson to form Alamo Neon in 1945. In Houston, C.V. Coppinger was just a shop helper at Texas Neon Sign Company when he started working there in 1937. After serving in the war, he returned to Houston to take over a bankrupt sign company, and turned it into a thriving, competitive business called State Sign Service. Also, one of the earliest Texas neon glass blowers since 1929, Dick Mitchell bought out Ft. Worth neon Sign Company after the war and created Texas Manufacturing Company, a leading neon sign producer and distributor in the southwest.

Immediately following the war, neon sign making was one of numerous vocational training programs in Texas created under the G.I. Bill. The government sponsored Louie Hoarel to teach neon sign glass blowing to ex servicemen at his shop in Amarillo. The Maurice Malone School in Denton was expressly designed with three shifts of productive training to teach hundreds of men the four basic neon tube bands that are required to make any neon sign. Between these two schools a new generation of neon sign makers was born in Texas who would later begin successful neon shops throughout the states. Raymond Hall, Bob Birth, and John Worthy are some of the Malone School graduates who formed competitive companies in Abilene, Midland, and Lubbock respectively. Truett Cargill and Bill Cox learned glass blowing from Hoarel at this time, and both are now presidents of major sign companies in the Panhandle (Cox bought out Hoarel Sign Company a few years after Louie Hoarel died in 1965).

It was easy for so many new neon shops to survive in Texas after the war because the demand for neon signs was so great. Also, the standardization of neon sign supplies effectively reduced costs and enabled production to skyrocket. Electrodes that were originally hand made, one at a time, are now mass produced and certainly more efficient. Many of the pre-war experimental glass tube varieties; Uranium Green, Beryllium White, and Helium White were discontinued when they were proven hazardous or inefficient, and the hard lead tubing: Ruby Red, Cobalt Blue, and Novil Gold were replaced with fluorescent powder coated tubing that was not only less expensive, but extended the range of available neon colors as well. The rare and inert gases that were once a prohibitive cost of neon sign making had become one of the cheapest commodities of the trade during these peak years.

Moreover, Texas neon advertising experienced its heyday in the late 1940's and early 1950's because so many of the old time neon sign men in the state were in the prime of their careers then.

Mass production techniques were perfected and exploited by the "super companies" in Texas. Zimmerman and Son, Texlite, McAx, and Texas Manufacturing Company incorporated stencil patterns, drilling templates, and other assorted devices enabling an assembly line production of neon signs for major advertising campaigns. These were in the country and as far away as Japan and Europe. In 1950, J.B. McMath and a close friend from Borich Sign Company, M.L. Vieregge designed and patented a $1500.00 portable machine that would facilitate any exacting bend in sheet metal sign construction. This so-called "McAx Roll" is still used extensively throughout the country.

Also originating in the design department of Texlite and McAx sign companies in Dallas are the most spectacular porcelain and neon theatre displays in Texas history. In every major city in Texas these landmark vestiges recall the glory of quintessential animated-neon expression that culminated during the peak years of neon sign making.

If it were not for the efforts of sign men who loved neon like Louie Hoarel in Amarillo, J.B. McMath in Dallas, Jules Lauve, Jr. in Galveston, and Bill Thomas in Abilene plastic signs would not have taken over in Texas as soon as they did. Despite detrimental weather conditions that have always threatened neon signs in Texas (i.e., hail storms in the Panhandle, wind storms in the west, and the salty gulf air in the south) these men overcame these obstacles and perpetuated neon signs as long as the market would bear. Downtown Amarillo was nationally applauded as "the Times Square of the High Plains" because of hundreds of Hoarel's beautiful neon signs that lighted Polk Street during this time. Jules Lauve, Jr. rose to fame with his many brilliant neon displays in and around Galveston (for which he used 'Vulcatex' putty to seal the electrodes against salt corrosion). He is especially noted for making the three enormous spectaculars on Galveston's Pleasure Pier in 1947, and his experimental 'candle light' neon lighting for the interior of Sam Maseo's Baliness Room Club in Galveston. Bill Thomas is another old-timer who loved neon. He came to Texas from California after the military service and set up a few neon shops before settling in Abilene in 1951. In the shadow of impending plastic signage, he is reported to have employed as many as eighty high-pressure salesmen at various times to promote neon sales in west Texas.

When the first Sky Hook hydraulic boom trucks were purchased in Texas to facilitate neon sign erection in the early 1950's, the introduction of plastic signs was imminent. The high-impact plastics that were developed by Rohm and Haas for airplane canopies during World War II were then developed and expanded for the Outdoor Advertising Company. The first vacuum-formed plastic signs with internal fluorescent light sources appeared in Texas in the early 1950's. Initially they were expensive signs, but their biggest selling feature was their low maintenance and resistance to hail and wind damage. Despite a growing public demand for plastic signs several prominent neon men refused to make or sell them at first. Nevertheless, as more and more neon sign companies began installing vacuum forming equipment the new trend in outdoor electric advertising was underway by 1955, and neon sign making in Texas subsided.

A genius appreciation of neon signs comes with the realization that each sign is a one-of-a-kind creation, from its design to its execution. Relative to the increasing mechanization of American industries, neon sign making is one of the few technologies that has remained virtually unchanged as a handcraft since its inception in the 1920's. The old-timers in the neon sign business have roots in the days of gold leaf and commercial sign artistry. They learned neon by trial and error, and they became the quality craftsmen. Neon sign lighting presented to them the single most creative, effective, and economical resource for transforming their wildest, most spectacular ideas into unique advertising displays.

The old-timers will agree that animated neon sign work was the most exciting electric advertising work that they ever had a part in, and they are sad to see it disappear. In the same breath they will contend that neon sign lighting will never vanish all together. Neon is inherently too efficient and brilliant to disregard as a thing of the past. Every trend in outdoor advertising always returns, they say, only disguised as something else. Even now, in the 1980's, architects and contemporary sculptors are exploiting the myriad potentials of neon sign lighting that began where neon sign makers left off.

Following the pattern of history, it is no wonder that neon sign making was replaced with a new trend. Trends rise till they peak, and then subside… for a while. The resources of neon sign making are still quite alive…just waiting for the outdoor advertising trend to turn again.

Chapter 6:

Taking Time to Help Someone by J.B. McMath Sr.

I had a very interesting experience one time while watching a sand lot ball game at Rivershon Park in Dallas, Texas.

I do not remember the exact date but it was a Saturday afternoon in 1946.

One of the teams engaged represented the Post Office, and Postmaster Howard Payne whom I knew, and spoke to was there to watch his team play.

I sat in the hot sun for a half hour or longer watching the two teams practice for the game and at the very instance the umpire called out "play ball" an inaudible voice spoke to my heart with greater force and clarity than had it been an ordinary audible voice.

The exact words of the voice were in the form of the following question, "What do you mean wasting your time here at this ball game when there are other things so much more important that you could be doing?"

The voice was so real and impressive that I moved the instant the last word was spoken.

I have never felt that I was committing a great sin attending a Saturday afternoon sand lot ball game that was free to the public.

However as you will see later God had an errand or duty for me to perform which required precision timing, and therefore the Holy Spirit had to speak very forcefully to me to prevent me from taking time to meditate before moving.

I got in my car and drove to the intersection of Maple Avenue where there was a boulevard stop sign, and as I stopped an old grey-headed, long whiskered, long and narrow, filthy looking man with a small bundle under his arm crept slowly across the intersection, and if I had been five or ten seconds later he would have already been across, and in either event I would not have seen him, hence God's precision timing.

Ordinarily I have very little sympathy for a person who doesn't choose to work if they can, however there was something about this man that attracted my attention and sympathy immediately.

He appeared to be very weak, undernourished, and sick, and I remarked to myself that man needs help; I watched to see where he was going and he sat down on the first park bench he came to.

The smallest amount of money I had was a $5.00 bill, and I told the Lord that I was going to the filling station at Maple and Oak Lawn to get it changed and if the man was still there when I returned I would take the circumstances to mean that he wanted me to help him.

When I returned he was still sitting where I last saw him and I parked my car and went over and spoke to him; he evidently thought I was one of the park officials and had come to chase him out of the park for he began immediately in a more or less apologetic manner to tell me all about himself.

I do not remember his name, but he said he was from Saint Joseph, Missouri, where he had been an employee of the city until he developed a hernia and had to quit his job. He still had the hernia and it was so large that it made him appear almost like a pregnant woman.

He said he had a sister living in Houston who wrote and told him if he would come to Houston she would take care of him. He said when he arrived there he found that she was neither physically or financially able to take care of him and that he was now on his way back home.

I asked him how he was traveling and he replied I am walking. I then asked him if that wasn't awfully hard on him, and he replied that the worst thing he had to endure was the mosquitos at night, that the walking was not so bad.

I also asked him if he could not catch a ride from time to time with someone to which he replied, "Oh no, no one will let me ride with them in my condition", and I could understand why.

He was about 70 years old and in his physical condition and the speed with which I observed that he could walk he must have been at least two months or more on the road from Houston to Dallas, which is some 250 miles, and he didn't appear to have had a shave, hair cut or bath since he left Houston, and not a change of clothing.

I asked him if he would ride the bus if someone would give him a ticket to St. Joseph, and he replied yes but then said, "I cannot ask or expect that much from anyone." I then asked him if he would accept a ticket from me and he gave the same answer.

I then invited him to get in my car and that I would take him to the bus station and buy him a ticket.

After starting for the bus station I felt that as a Christian I should by all means witness to him and also tell him how the Lord had led me to him.

I approached him by asking him if he was a Christian, and he replied yes, and with a ring of sincerity he said, "I have my Bible with me," I asked to see it and to my surprise the larger portion of that bundle under his arm was a beautiful Bible, the only clean thing he had, for he kept it wrapped up in a tarpaulin which he evidently used to sleep on.

He said his Bible was the only comfort he had and that he tried to stop each evening early enough to see to read it before he had prayer and lay down for the night. He also said he was a member of the Church of God.

I took him to the bus station and bought him a ticket, and sat him down as close to the ticket seller as I could and asked the man in charge if he would see that no one molested him and that he boarded the St. Joseph bus. He assured me he would.

I gave him some money with which to buy food and told him goodbye.

Now I am sure that many after reading this document will say that I had just wasted time, affections, and money on an unworthy tramp, and if I didn't know the circumstances I might say the same thing for it is hard to understand how anyone could walk four or five miles a day for two months and not be able to take a bath in a creek somewhere, but God knows the reason and I accept it on that basis.

I believe that one of the things that contributed to his condition was the fact that he was trying to make it on his own without calling on anyone for help, he gave not the least evidence that he was a deadbeat or an imposter but a poor and no doubt unwise Christian whose prayers God had answered.

I know that the Spirit of God spoke to me at the ball game, and I believe he directed this entire affair from start to finish, and I am grateful to God that he saw fit to honor me with this inspiring assignment, all of which was no doubt an answer to this mans prayers for help.

J.B. McMath, Sr.

Chapter 7

H.H. Wineburgh (previous owner of Texlite) The Story of Texlite taken from the periodical Texlite News, 15 May. 1951

Prelude: I think it is interesting to note that Mr. Wineburgh was given the Texlite Electric Sign Company as a graduation present from Yale.

In the summer of 1924, Georges Claude, a renowned French inventor, introduced a new type of electrical advertising to the city of Paris. He had discovered that by pumping neon gas into a tube and charging it with high voltage electricity, an orange red glow would result. The use of neon tubes spread like wild fire throughout France and on to other parts of the continent. At the end of the summer, while returning from a trip to Europe, the writer met a Mr. Hollingsworth who was the representative of the Claude Neon Company, the company that had built neon signs throughout France and, indeed, the rest of Europe. Mr. Hollingsworth was on his way to the United States to make arrangements to have this type of display manufactured and sold in this country. During the voyage I attempted to contract with Claude Neon for the exclusive manufacture of neon signs in the five Southwestern states, but the demands made were so far beyond the capabilities of Texlite at that time that nothing was accomplished.

I could not get the idea of neon out of my mind, however. There was no question that the possibilities were enormous, and I was anxious to see Texlite enter this new field. At that time I was living on 84th Street and Madison Avenue in New York City, and one evening as I was walking home from work down 84th, a sign in a brownstone private home, quite far into the poorer neighborhood caught my attention. The little sign, which read "X-Ray," was apparently made on the same principal as neon.

On investigation, I learned that this sign had been made by an electrical engineer, Ray Machlett, a graduate of Cornell University. His father had been in the X-ray tube manufacturing business, and Mr. Machlett, who was a very young man, had apparently done some experimenting on his own. He was of the opinion that his product did not infringe upon the Claude Neon patent inasmuch as he had not employed the same principle. Under the Claude patent, the electrode had to be a minimum of 1.5 square decimeters per ampere with low pressure used in the tube. Mr. Machlett used a smaller electrode with higher pressure in the tube.

After considerable negotiating, my father, a few friends, and I formed a small company in New York called TUBELIGHT, INC., and sold signs made by Mr. Machlett. These were small, simple signs for florists, barbershops, cafes, etc. In 1927 I took the first neon sign west of the Mississippi River to St. Louis, carrying it in a Pullman berth. It was placed in the window of Grimm and Gorley, prominent St. Louis florists, and read simply, "Say It With Flowers." The sign created such excitement that people poured in to see it, and it was only a matter of a few hours before their enthusiasm in handling it resulted in much broken glass.

In March 1928, Texlite bought out Tubelight and started manufacturing neon signs in its own plant. To the best of our knowledge, the first two neon signs erected in the city of Dallas were "PAUL'S SHOES" and "ZINKE'S FINE SHOE REPAIR," At this writing, we are still making signs for Paul's Shoes.

In the meantime, Texlite's electric sign business was on the upsurge. I had become president of the company following Mr. Pickett's death in 1926, and early in 1927 we were commissioned to build one of the largest electric signs that had ever been erected in the Southwest. This was to be for the Saenger Theatre in New Orleans. The sign was built in our factory and on completion it was found to be too large to get out of the building.

It was necessary to take down the entire front of the building in order to deliver the sign.

Neon was becoming popular in the Southwest, and its use was spreading in both the North and East. It was decided larger quarters were necessary, and the company moved to 4112 Commerce Street, not far from Fair Park. A Texlite office was also opened in Atlanta, Georgia, and one in Houston, and we stationed a salesman in St. Louis. During the next three or four years, Texlite enjoyed an excellent electric and neon sign business and had salesmen traveling throughout the Southwest. Our theatre signs and outdoor displays were among the finest in the entire region. One of these was a solid copper sign for the Fox Theatre in Atlanta, which, I believe, is still hanging today in the same location.

We had a rather interesting experience in the Southeast. The company had sold a number of neon signs in Atlanta and one of our salesmen there sold a sign to the National Garage in Birmingham. This was the first neon sign sold in Birmingham, and when the sign hangers attempted to erect it, the power company who declined to permit the sign to be displayed stopped them. Their contention was that since a transformer was used, the sign actually consumed twice as much electricity as reflected by the meter, and consequently half the revenue would be lost. After considerable persuasion, and with the assistance of the Georgia Power Company, we were able to show the Alabama Power Company that, admitting their contention to be true, they would nevertheless actually increase their profits because of the increase in the number of signs that would certainly come into use.

During the late '20's, porcelain enamel had become a popular finish for sign faces, and was becoming increasingly important as a finish for electric and neon signs. Texlite had been buying its porcelain enamel in the East, in the Chicago area, and even on the Pacific Coast and it was difficult to obtain satisfactory deliveries from such distant points. Moreover, the enamel in those days was applied very heavily and chipped easily, so that many shipments arrived in poor condition. Under the circumstances, and in spite of the fact business was beginning to show a decline following the stock market crash of October, 1929, it was decided to install a porcelain enamel furnace and complimentary equipment. The first oven was turned on the latter part of 1930, and Texlite became the first porcelain enameling plant south of Chicago, east of Los Angeles, and west of Nashville.

J.B. on the far right, sitting down.

LIGHT LITERATURE

THE inside of this booklet shows a few of our many installations thruout the 48 states of our country. Grant it more than a passing glance—you will find the time well spent.

The specimens shown were chosen at random, out of an immense accumulation of photographs. There are no "preferred jobs" for this organization. No matter what size or kind it may be, each order is treated as tho our reputation were staked upon the result.

Copyright 1930
TEXLITE ELECTRIC SIGN COMPANY, INC.
U. S. A.

1930

TEXLITE boasts of serving several of the nation's largest oil companies with their electric sign requirements.

Displays such as these greet the motorist on highways and boulevards. A splendid combination of attractiveness and sturdiness.

A brilliant red Neon border outlines the Atlantic sign.

THE TEXLITE IDEA

THE duty of your Electrical Display is to attract the passerby's attention. To do its best for you it must be endowed with every faculty which makes for greater strength of impression, for better harmony of appeal.

Your electric sign cannot talk back! Once its impression is made, it must stand or fall,—frequently your own standing may be misjudged by its appearance.

TEXLITE will breathe life into your Electric Sign, will impart the strength of better grooming, the confidence-inspiring appeal of business dignity.

For many years TEXLITE has been building an organization of highly trained artists, engineers, skilled mechanics and intelligent representatives to sell, lease and maintain Neon and all other types of Electric Displays which best fit the needs of their customers.

TEXLITE has only ONE incentive— "To build quality signs at the lowest possible cost."

THE SAENGER THEATRE
"A Public Theatre"
New Orleans, Louisiana

New Orleans theatregoers appreciate the attractiveness of the beautiful Saenger illumination. Clear, white letters set in an animated background predominate within a running border of brilliantly colored lights, with a spectacular bursting effect at the top

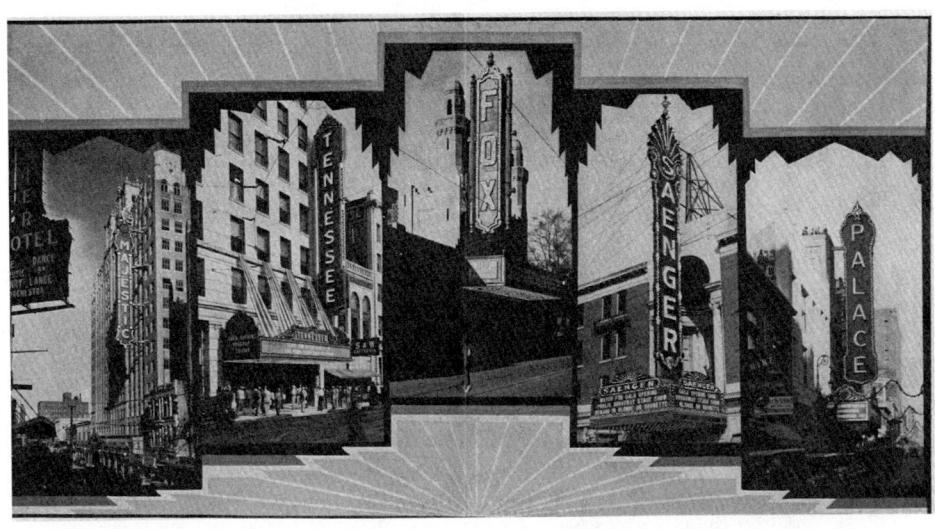

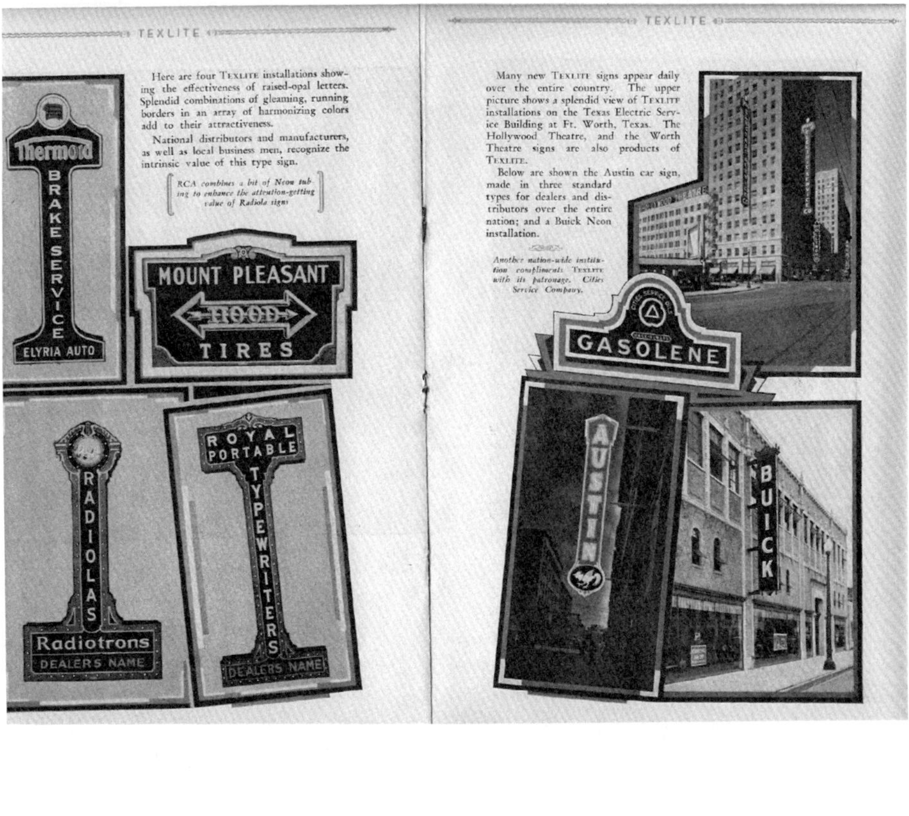
TEXLITE

Here are four TEXLITE installations showing the effectiveness of raised-opal letters. Splendid combinations of gleaming, running borders in an array of harmonizing colors add to their attractiveness.

National distributors and manufacturers, as well as local business men, recognize the intrinsic value of this type sign.

RCA combines a bit of Neon tubing to enhance the attention-getting value of Radiola signs

TEXLITE

Many new TEXLITE signs appear daily over the entire country. The upper picture shows a splendid view of TEXLITE installations on the Texas Electric Service Building at Ft. Worth, Texas. The Hollywood Theatre, and the Worth Theatre signs are also products of TEXLITE.

Below are shown the Austin car sign, made in three standard types for dealers and distributors over the entire nation; and a Buick Neon installation.

Another nation-wide institution compliments TEXLITE with its patronage. Cities Service Company.

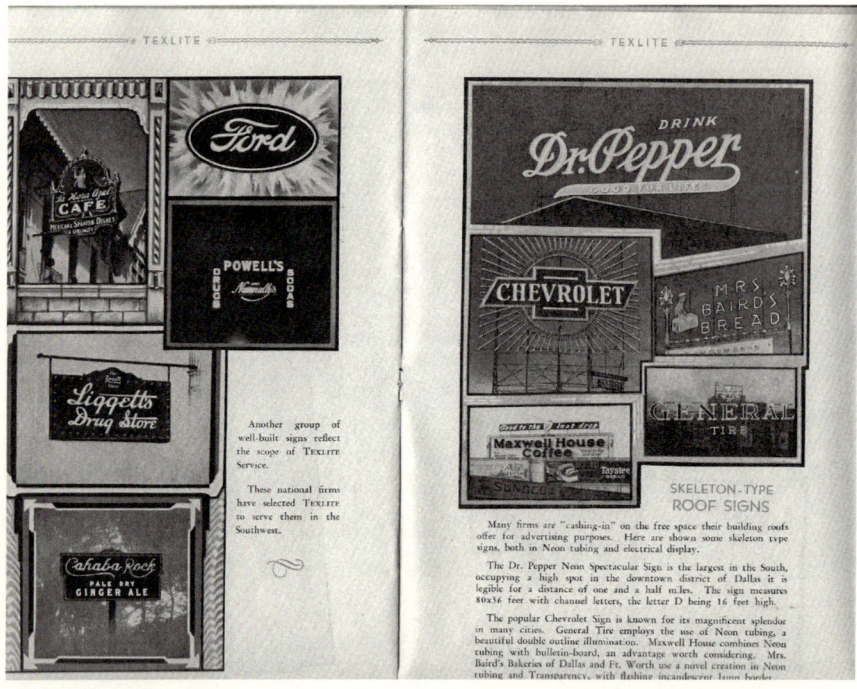

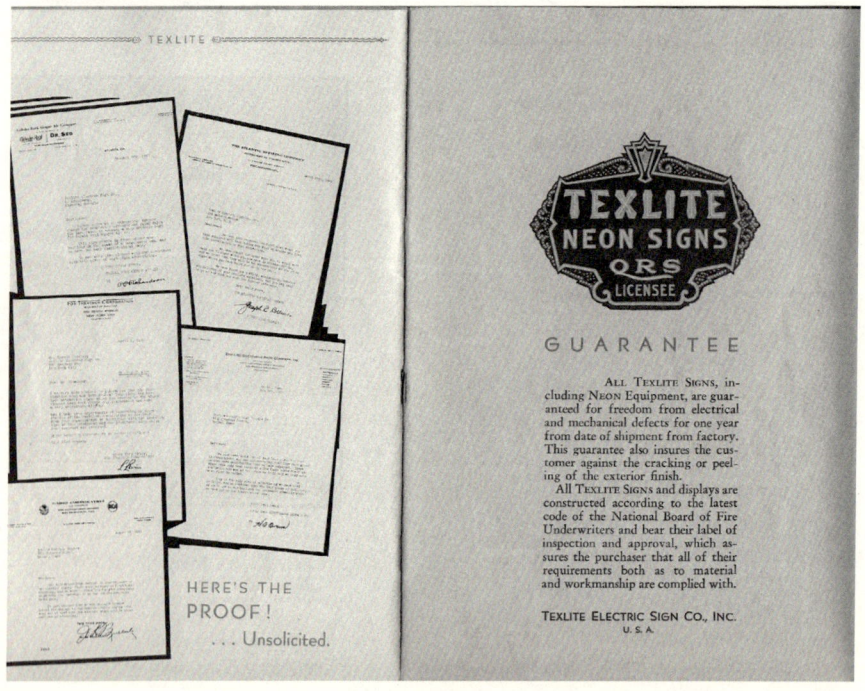

J.B. McMath, sitting far right

Example of porcelain service station.

Example of porcelain service station.

TIME AND TEXLITE MARCH ON! Here are 14 gentlemen who have served the company 20 years or more and are still going strong. Back row, left to right: B. F. Hamman, Dale McMath, Walter Guernsey, Harold Guernsey, Arthur Reno, W. C. Cain. Front row, left to right: Cammon Slocum, Joe Padilla, Sam McMath, H. W. McMahan, H. H. Wineburgh, Reuben Freeman, Carl L. Bishop, and Henry Nelson.

TURN BACK THE OLD PORCELAIN ENAMEL CLOCK! This picture was taken in 1923, the year H. H. Wineburgh purchased the Texlite Electric Sign Co. Top man, behind the ladder is Marteen Vieregge. Standing, middle row; left to right: Claude Winburn (now outstanding Dallas physician); Frank C. Hibbetts; Walter Vieregge; Pickney McMath (now with Matteson-Southwest, Houston); Jack Hendricks; Sam McMath (superintendent of metal fabrication); Dale McMath (chief pattern maker); Roy Crabtree; Ed Jones (deceased); Bill Seago; Robert L. Slocum (now with Federal Sign Co., in Dallas); Ran Jones; J. B. McMath (partner in the McAx Corp.); Erwin Reisser (deceased); Miss Katherine Jones (only woman general manager in Texlite history); J. C. Pickett (deceased—son-in-law of P. S. Borich, founder of the company); Wilbur Sweden; Peter S. Borich (deceased—started the business in 1879). Seated: Alvin Vieregge (owner of Flo-Lite Neon Sign Co., Big Spring, Texas), Tom Freeman, W. P. Slocum, name unknown, and Arthur Chapman. Note the old Model "T" Ford truck in the background!

Chapter 8

Relationship with J.J. "Jack Axilrod" Business Partner by J.B. McMath

Mr. Axilrod was an orthodox Jew, and myself a Gentile Christian, however, the wide difference in our religious belief interfered in no way with our harmonious relationship; in fact I could honestly elaborate on our congenial association so that it would sound unbelievable to those who were not experimentally aware of the fact.

I have never met a more open minded, unbiased person. I was always confident that God had joined he and I together as business associates.

One time Jack made a trip to New York on very important company business and before leaving he gave me his itinerary and it called for a return trip by Detroit. The next day the president of the company came by the office and asked me why I agreed to let him come back by Detroit, and I answered by saying, "He is our sales manager and by my personal observation of his work I have found that his judgment is right so often and wrong so seldom that I find it good judgment on my part to let him do just about as he pleases," and I said further that "knowing him as I do if I should try to regiment him and require my personal approval of all his actions, we may as well fire him, for it would absolutely kill his spirit of enthusiasm and confidence in the company." With that statement, the matter was closed.

I have known only one man in my 45 years of association with our type of business that could sell as much while traveling full time, as Jack could sell over the telephone alone. After he once made the acquaintance of a customer, he did most of his further selling to him over the phone, especially out of town customers. I have heard him talk many times to some of the biggest corporate executives in the country, and from their conversation you would think they had known each other all their lives. Early after America's entry into World War II Mr. Axilrod was in a serious auto accident in which he broke his hip bone and was laid up for eight months, and naturally we kept him on the pay roll. However, he only drew a very moderate salary, and had depended on his commissions for his principal income. With his sudden loss to the company at a time when we were attempting to convert to war or defense work, we had no easy time getting adjusted to the circumstances. Our president employed a sales engineer, who was supposed to be familiar with aircraft instruction as well as acquainted with some of the top executives in the industry, and the two of them made numerous trips to various aircraft plants in an attempt to secure sub contract business, but to no avail. I personally wrote a letter to our various sales representatives and asked them to call on every defense plant in the area and to observe what they were doing and if they found anything that they felt we could do to offer a quote on it. Our Houston man went to Beaumont and called on the Pennsylvania shipyards and found four mine sweepers being built for the Navy needing someone to build and install the air conditioning ducts, etc. in them. We bid the job at around $100,000 and got it. It was the most complicated job we had ever undertaken but we did an excellent job and were on schedule. There were two other contractors doing similar work in the yard at the same time on cargo boats, but they were much larger and not nearly as complicated and when the shipyard got ready to place an order for duct work on an additional 14 cargo boats, these other two contractors advised the shipyards that our company was too new and inexperienced to undertake this same type of work on the cargo vessels, but the general manager of the shipyard operation told me personally that the reason they gave us the mine sweeper job was because it was so complicated and the other two contractors were afraid of it and didn't want the responsibility. He further stated, "You not only have done the finest job in the shipyards on similar work but you have been the most congenial and cooperative contractor in the yard." To make a long story short we received an order for seven of the cargo boats as a result of our standing in this yard, we had no difficulty in finding open doors for our proposals in other defense plants through the country for anything in the industry that we felt we could do.

Our operation became so large in Beaumont that it necessitated our opening of a sub plant there, and we re-hired a former employee who was then with a company in Memphis, Tennessee to manage this sub plant for us. It seemed to everyone by this time that we had finally made the grade and had little to worry about.

One day "Jack" as we called him, asked Mac, "Does the Lord prosper this company because of me a Jew or because of you a Christian?" I replied, "The Lord prospers this company because of both of us." Jack accompanied me a number of times to various Christian church services and was always a liberal contributor to the offering. We always prayed together over our problems, business and otherwise, and one morning we had a problem that merited unified prayer, and he came into my office and said, 'Mac, let's pray over our problem.' As we knelt to pray he asked me to lead; now up until this time we had prayed silently, but I decided to pray audibly and when I had finished he says, "Mac, you didn't pray right, you didn't pray in Jesus name." You see he had just attended several Christian services with me, and every prayer he had heard ended in Jesus name. He said, "You were afraid that I being a Jew you might offend me by praying in Jesus name," and he admonished, 'Don't you ever do that again, but always pray in the name of your God, Jesus Christ.'

Jack had two serious heart attacks during the first ten years we were in business together, the last one being fatal.

He fell as he was leaving the office one day just before we had been in business together one month, and was hospitalized for five months. I had left for Houston the day before, taking my wife with me, to spend a week calling on customers and potential customers, and the first one I called on informed me that my office was trying to reach me. I immediately called and learned what had happened, but was informed that the doctor would divulge no information concerning his ailment or condition. With such vague information I instructed our office to call the doctor and tell him that I was to be in Houston one week and that I must know about Mr. Axilrod's ailment and condition as to weather or not it would be all right for me to continue my weeks schedule in Houston.

My wife and I went back to our hotel room and awaited the return call and at two p.m. we were told what had happened, and were informed that it was extremely serious and that his two sons had been called home from Boston where they were attending school, and for me to return to Dallas immediately. With this information, my wife suggested we pray for him, and we both knelt and prayed that God would spare his life.

It was two or three months later before Jack was allowed to have visitors or talk, and when I did get to see him, he voluntarily informed me that he was very near death when he got to the hospital but he was impressed by the Lord that he was going to let him live.

Several months later I went to the same doctor for a checkup and his nurse brought up the subject of Mr. Axilrod and she said, "You know when we took him in that day his blood pressure was so low that we doubted he would leave the office alive."

I asked her what time of day that was and she replied 2:30 p.m. You will recall it was between 2:00 and 2:30 p.m. the same day that we prayed for him.

Some might wonder why God didn't raise him up right then if he touched him as we very definitely believed he did, but it was several years later before I was made to understand why, and the answer is too personal to put in writing.

Soon after we held our annual directors meeting and the president suggested in the meeting that we cut Jack off the payroll until he got well. I spoke up and said, "If we cut this man off our payroll we will ruin and likely loose the best salesman and one of the most conscientious workers this company has ever had and I don't agree with the idea at all." He then suggested that our attorney talk to Jack and get him to sign a release to the company relieving them of any liability arising from his accident. I felt I had already said about all I should say in opposition to his plans, however, I did casually say that would hurt him. Jack never told me but I learned later from one of the directors present at the meeting that he had told Jack everything that had transpired at the meeting. This information then helped me to understand Jack's changed attitude towards the company after his recovery and return to work. However, Jack never did as long as he lived say that he knew of the incident. Just before his recovery the president and myself drove to Beaumont by way of Houston to pick up our area representative for more or less an inspection of the Beaumont operation and everything was found to be going well and a reasonable profit being made and a sizable backing of orders on hand. This offered me a somewhat secure feeling for at least the immediate future and the president seemed to have the false impression that my only interest in Jack was that I thought he was indispensable to the company and he seemed to think that now since the company was doing well without him I might be willing to change my mind and might be willing to let him go. So on our way back to Houston he asked me the same identical question about him that he had asked before, namely, "Mac, what are you going to do with Jack?" and I says, "I am going to keep him and when he gets up I am going to send him to the aircraft industry, and if anyone can get some business from them, he can." I turned to our area representative and asked, "Don't you agree with that?" And he replied, "I believe you are right." As another indication that Jack had been told of the incident at the directors meeting, just two weeks later he got out of bed and on crutches called the office to send him a driver to drive him all over Fort Worth to call on Consolidated Aircraft Company and in less than one month from his first call we had orders for aircraft work, and before the war was over we were working the Dallas plant around the clock on aircraft work. When the war ended we had over six million dollars in unfilled orders for the aircraft work alone. Jack sold every pennies worth of this business and I feel he did it just to prove himself and vindicate my faith in him. One month we made $50,000 in what we considered excess profit and we mailed a check for that amount without their knowing that we had made it or were even expecting it.

The Lord spoke to my heart one day and impressed me to believe it was a psalm that would open Jack's heart if I would read it to him. The thought blessed my heart every time I thought about it, but they're being over 1000 pages in the Bible with 150 psalms alone, and to find that scripture without a miracle from God seemed impossible. However, I believed he would reveal it to me at the right time.

Jack and I often talked about the salvation of Jesus Christ and the Christian religion, and he always seemed sincerely interested, however, I could tell almost every time we discussed the subject that someone had talked to him against the Christian religion.

One time I walked into his office and he says, "Mac, if Christ did all the things ascribed to him in the New Testament, why do the Jews not have similar records available?" To which I replied, "Jack, I could send out a call by television or newspaper and invite every person in Dallas who had been healed by faith in Jesus Christ to meet at some appointed place to give a testimony and I venture to say we could have at least 1000 with physical healing of about every disease and physical ailment known to medical science, but did you ever read anything about these in the local newspapers? No, and you never will."

Jack and I were associated together for nine years while I was the general manager, and he the sales manager for Texlite Inc. It was during this nine years of association that I gained a good understanding of him and of his fine attributes and qualities, resulting in no hesitancy on my part of considering him as a companion in a business venture. I was at the time 51 years old, the same as his age, and had been thinking for some time of trying to get into something that offered more security. The company had no retirement or pension plan and knowing of the treatment that Jack would have had to face had it not been for me did not at all enhance my faith in a safe or favorable future with the company. I knew that my future was no more secure than my strength, physical and mental capacity would merit, so I naturally had an open ear and an open mind to what Jack had to say about it. I also felt that I had reached the age in life when I must do something for the security of self and family soon or it would be too late. As a result we became very serious in our discussions. However, being fully aware that my success and position with the company had been the direct results of the mercy and directions of Almighty God himself whom I served and prayed morning and night for his help and guidance. I determined that I would make no move until I had the assurance of his will in the matter. The wide difference in our two religious beliefs did not prevent us from developing a true mutual confidence and friendship unsurpassed in my knowledge except possibly where two close blood relatives were involved.

However, since this was the most important business decision of my life, and since I had not made an important decision during the entire thirty years I had been a Christian, without first praying, I certainly did not want to make an exception this time, so I made it a matter of sincere prayer.

Naturally for two top salaried men in a corporation to embark on a business venture, and expect to earn any kind of a livelihood to begin with, they must have some facilities, especially when they are going to have to compete with the fine facilities they are leaving and a company known the nation over for quality and service.

There was a small company in Dallas at that time which had closed down during what was then known as World War II. This facility was for sale for $35,000 and I had known of at least three friends who had negotiated with the owner to buy the property, but in each case the deal fell through when the owner demanded in each case that they put up $15,000 to insure against failure for lack of operating capital. His reason for this was that he did not want all cash for the business, but mostly in the form of an interest-bearing note over a ten-year period so naturally I prayed very earnestly about the matter. I just prayed a very simple prayer just like I was talking to someone about a business proposition but with an earnest desire and faith for an answer. I went to work for the parent company of which the present one was a part in June 1917, and it was at my suggestion that this latter company was established in the winter of 1922. I built the first building they ever operated in, and became its first superintendent and employee. The company was sold in 1924, and was incorporated that same year. I purchased approximately 6% of the capital stock at the time of incorporation and was elected to the original board, and was later elected treasurer and made an officer of this company. I was made general manager in 1935, and upon the death of the father and co-owner with the son of the business I was elected vice president in his place, and shortly after that I was made executive vice president and chairman of the board. The president owned the controlling interest in the business and could naturally do most anything he desired in the election of officers and directors, and about six months before I left the company he informed me that he was going to make me president and himself chairman of the board, but we were both working on government approved salaries and our attorney advised against this move until after the war was over, fearing that this might indicate a lessening of responsibility on his part and a reduction in salary.

We bought the company, however and before approaching the owner I prayed, and the answer was yes.

We both announced our resignations immediately to the president of the company; this was early in December 1945, and to become effective January 1, 1946. I was offered a 25% increase in salary to stay, however, I was so convinced that I was in God's will that I refused the offer.

Chapter 9

The History of the McAx Corporation as written by J.B. McMath, Sr.

The McAx Corporation had its beginning January 1, 1946 through its acquisition of the Ra-Lite Sign Company, located at 628 Third Avenue, Dallas, Texas. The Ra-Lite Sign Company was a non-incorporated concern and was established around 1920, by the late Harry H. Sellers, and J.B. McMath and J.J. Axilrod purchased it.

Ra-Lite started as an electric sign manufacturer and later engaged in the manufacture of luminous tube or neon signs and in the late 30's, added small porcelain enamel signs. The company remained very small during its entire existence, but always showed a profit under the very conservative management of its founder. The Ra-Lite Company ceased operations at the beginning of World War II, because of the restricted use of crucial materials, and never reopened until purchased by McMath-Axilrod, after the end of the war. It was then incorporated under the laws of Texas, and the name changed to McMath-Axilrod Corporation.

The properties purchased by Ra-Lite consisted of some 18,750 square feet of land area with building covering 9,400 square feet and included the electric sign and porcelain enameling equipment belonging to the company. The buildings were very inadequate, and in great need of repairs and alterations. Most of the equipment was of poor quality and obsolete, and while the total price was only $35,000 it is doubtful that the purchasers would have had it at any price, should better facilities have been available; but the shortage of materials and equipment created by the war made the purchase of better facilities impossible.

It was the new owners objective to continue, but on a much larger scale, the manufacture of the same type of products as that of the original company, and to add new items as demand and adaptability through research were justified. As a result of this policy, the original product, which consisted of 100% of the company's volume, was now only about 30%. The other 70% consisted of new developments and new lines, and the percentage is still growing toward the new times.

The following is a list of the company's main items as produced today:

1. PORCELAIN ENAMEL PRODUCTS:
   - (A.) Architectural porcelain enamel known as curtain wall construction for multiple story buildings, sold to the building industry.
   - (B.) Porcelain enamel veneer or fascia for new buildings and for re-facing of old buildings, particularly service stations, sold to the building industry and individuals.
   - (C.) A standard pre-fabricated porcelain enamel building for which patents are pending, primarily for service stations, and sold to the oil companies.
   - (D.) Porcelain enamel portable service stations, sold to the oil industry.
   - (E.) Porcelain enamel signs and identification letters sold to the building industry and individuals.
   - (F.) Porcelain enamel jobbing work for concerns requiring enameling from time to time who do not have such facilities of their own.
   - (G.) Porcelain enamel sign faces and letters for the electric sign industry.

2. VARIOUS TYPES OF ILLUMINATED SIGNS:
   - (A.) Neon or luminous tube signs with all porcelain enamel bodies, both spectacular and semi-spectacular for national concerns and individuals.
   - (B.) Indirectly illuminated plastic signs for the same class and for the same customers.

(C.) Combination neon and plastic signs for the same class and for the same customers.

(D.) Sign Maintenance for the same class and for the same customers.

3. MISCELLANEOUS ITEMS

(A.) All types of fabricated sign poles for the oil industry.

(B.) Two types of metal forming machines for the sign and porcelain enamel industry.

(C.) A power letter brake for the sign and porcelain enamel industry.

The corporation was chartered January 14, 1946, for a period of fifty years for the purpose of transacting a manufacturing business, with an authorized capitol stock of $30,000 divided into 300 shares of common stock, with the par value of $100 each; 150 shares were subscribed and paid for at time of incorporation as follows: J.B. McMath, 60 shares, J.J. AxIlrod, 60 shares, and Charles P. Reese, 30 shares. Minutes of a special stockholders meeting June 5, 1947, acknowledges payment of $15,000 for the remaining 150 shares, by the original stockholders and in the same ratio of ownership. J.B. McMath was elected president, J.J. AxIlrod, vice-president, and Charles F. Reese, secretary and treasurer. These three also constituted the first board of directors. Since Charles F. Reese operated a supply business to which McMath-AxIlrod became competitive, he decided to resign his office as secretary treasurer on June 29, 1948. His duties of treasurer were added to those of the president, and his duties of secretary were added to those of the vice-president, making the president, president-treasurer, and the vice-president, secretary.

The charter was amended on December 17, 1948, to allow increase in capital from $30,000 to 65,000 with the full amount being subscribed for, with $47,500 paid in. On January 23, 1950, the charter was amended again, to allow increase in capital stock from 465,000 to 125,000 paid in. September 27, 1951, the charter was amended again to allow increase in capital stock from $125,000 to $225,000 the full amount being subscribed for and with $200,000 paid in. October 25, 1953, the charter was amended to allow reduction of stock from $225,000 to $200,000. Cancelling the unissued stock did this.

Mr. J.J. Axilrod, who had never fully recovered from a very serious heart attack, which occurred about one month after the company was established, passed away on January 29, 1956. At his death, the company purchased the remaining 364 shares. The price paid was $137.50 per share. This was slightly above book value. The total purchase price being $110,000.

On December 12, 1957, or approximately 10 months after the death of Mr. Axilrod, the directors voted to change the name of the company from McMath-Axilrod Corporation to McAx Corporation; hence, the company's name today. At a special meeting of the stockholders and directors, following Mr. Axilrod's death, Mrs. Evelyn R. Robinson, who had appointed the Axilrod's estate's executrix, was elected to fill Mr. Axilrod's place of director. She resigned, however, as soon as she had disposed of the Axilrod stock, and since we already had two vice-presidents, J.B. McMath, Jr., and G. Walter Gray, we did not elect anyone to take Mr. Axilrod's place at that time. However, Mrs. Joe H. Marichum was elected treasurer to fill Mr. Axilrod's place as secretary. The present directors and officers are as follows:

J. B. McMath, Sr., President, Treasurer, and Director

J. B. McMath, Jr., Executive Vice-President, and Director

G. Walter Gray, Vice-President and Director

Mrs. Joe Markham, Secretary and Director

V. Patrick Chandler, Vice-President and Director

C. F. Reece, Director

W. C. Scurry, Director

All of the foregoing stock increases were made possible only through stock dividends or the re-investment of portions of owner's salaries. There were no other alternatives to this procedure for the simple reason that the company started with a very limited capital and very inadequate facilities. Naturally, the tremendous backlog of demand created by the war made it possible to get by with most any kind of facilities while this great demand lasted. However, it did not take a Soloman to foresee that this Utopia, or non-competitive age, so to speak, would not last forever. At least two adverse circumstances were inevitable and would eventually have to be met, namely, keen competition and higher labor costs. To prepare for this sure eventuality, we felt that there was but one alternative. That was to add more and better facilities. More facilities in order to reduce overhead percentage wise, by doing a larger volume of business, and better facilities in order to improve quality product wherever possible, and at the same time improve efficiency in plant operation, thereby reducing man hours per unit to help compensate for the eventual increase in wage rates which were sure to come. It is in pursuance of this policy that the stockholders have raised capital stock of the company from time to time and re-invested earnings in the business.

The company operated at its original location, 628 Third Avenue, for fifteen years, or from January 1946 until January 1961. During this time they added 37,500 square feet of land area to the original 18,700 square feet of land, giving a final total of 50,250 square feet of land area and 47,800 feet was added to the original 9400 square feet of floor space giving us a final total of 57,250 square feet of floor space at the time the property was taken over by the State Highway Department. A portion of the buildings were two stories high, which accounts for the floor space being slightly greater than that of the land area. During all of this time, modern machinery was added just as fast as finances would permit, and fortunately the company, as a result of this policy, was able to keep sufficiently abreast meeting, as well as in many cases, surpassing its competition. The trends in the porcelain enamel industry has changed so radically during the past fifteen years that much of the equipment and knowledge required to operate today was hardly heard of at that time. We are now dealing, to a very great extent, with a highly intelligent clientele, which includes the architect, the engineer, and the building industry, a profession and industry who wants the best and who are best qualified to know it when they see it. When McAx learned in early 1958 that its property would eventually be absorbed by the new R. L. Thornton expressway, they began immediately to search for suitable property for relocating, and since no suitable improved facilities could be located, we finally decided on a very desirable building site consisting of some six and three quarter acres at the corner of MKT Railroad and Overton Road in South Dallas. This land was purchased for $24,000 cash. By the time the Highway Department began to negotiate for the purchase of the property on Third Avenue, we had found that it would require approximately one-half million dollars to build suitable buildings, buy new ovens, and relocate our facilities on our new location. We also found that after this expenditure, we would have very little if any room than at Third Avenue, where our crowded quarters were already hindering production and efficiency, so we gave up the idea of building and were contemplating liquidation, when it was brought to our attention that the Rheems plant at McGregor was for sale. We contacted them immediately, and after receiving their offer, made them a counter offer, which they accepted. The Rheems consisted of a main manufacturing building with some 120,000 square feet of floor space; slightly double that of our Third Avenue property in Dallas. The property is served by two main line railroads, namely, the Santa Fe and the Cotton Belt; 124 and 7/10 acres of land with the largest continuous enameling oven in the south and southwest. Its replacement costs by its builders is estimated at $155,000. After spending $30,000 for a complete rebuilding job, it is now in practically new condition. Our ovens at Dallas were the box type and far less economical to operate especially where volume production is required, and produces an inferior quality of work to that of the continuous oven. Our original cost of the McGregor property was $76,000. However, to date we have spent a total of $293,000 on the property, including several pieces of new equipment, which is approximately $100,000 more than we contemplated spending at the beginning. However, we found this absolutely necessary and feel that it was well spent. The company now has a plant that is very conservatively appraised at $750,000, and a dream, which we have had for some fifteen years, is now realized. These new and larger facilities with ample storage and floor space will enable us to push to the very limits for the first time, our pre-fabricated building program that requires much more room than was available at our previous location because of the necessity of building stations in quantities and storing them in advance of erection.

It has also been our desire for many years to go into the sign pole manufacturing business, but never had sufficient space available for such an operation. Since moving to McGregor, we have already shipped a thousand poles with new orders for 250 more. They average more than $150 each. The first order for these poles did not prove profitable from a labor and material standpoint, however, the experience gained was invaluable. Naturally, we had to set up a department and train personnel in an altogether new operation. We now have 250 additional poles to make at a 10% increase in price, and our cost records show that we are now making a normal profit in regard to labor. We find that many of the McGregor people are of German heritage and very technically inclined. Most of them were raised in this community, do not wish to leave, and are therefore very desirable employees.

Chapter 10

The Story of the Magnolia Building from the book The Unauthorized History of Dallas, Texas by Rose-Mary Rumbley, 1991.

Pegasus and Mobil Oil

"It's a great peg driven into the ground holding Dallas in its place from no matter which direction the town is approached." A very enthusiastic journalist made this statement as he looked at the Magnolia Oil Building, when it opened, August 14, 1922, corner of Commerce and Akard. For us natives the Magnolia Oil Building of 29 stories was the grandest and most imposing edifice in the Southwest. It made Dallas a city.

The Magnolia Petroleum Company was the producer of Socony and later, Mobile Petroleum products. Magnolia was a pioneering force in the oil industry starting as a series of smaller companies. Actually, it rose from the Spindletop find near Beaumont, one of the greatest discoveries ever made.

That oil was discovered when Patillo Higgins, a super tough guy from Beaumont who suddenly got religion, took his Baptist Sunday school class out on a picnic near some springs on a hill called Spindletop. The rainbow colors in the water and the smell of that water convinced Higgins that there was oil. He finally got enough money together to drill and on January 10, 1901, the big 'un came in and the world has never been the same. Dallas certainly wasn't the same, especially when Magnolia decided to make the city its corporate headquarters. It is interesting that both Spindletop and McAx were started providentially.

Sir Alfred Charles Bossum, internationally known architect, author, critic, and statesman, born in 1881, a Baron in the British nobility, designed the building. He was trained at the St. Thomas School and the Architectural School of the Royal Academy of the Arts. He established offices in New York in 1903 and in the years to follow became very well known throughout the world as a builder of grand buildings. His Dallas Renaissance design cost 4 million dollars to build in the early 1920's. Every office has an outside view built by the design following the "court construction" method. There are Italian marble floors and American walnut woodwork. There are 500 offices and 16 elevators. The whole point of the building was to establish Dallas as an oil capital and the building certainly did this.

Then, the icing on the cake came twelve years later, November 8, 1934. Pegasus, the flying red horse, the symbol for Magnolia Oil, was placed on top. Whenever I take anyone of a tour of Dallas, I always point out that there are actually two horses up in this "one horse town." Actually, it was necessary to have two horses so that the wind wouldn't blow the beloved figure down.

In 1934, the American Petroleum Institute Convention was held in Dallas. Magnolia Oil went to Texlite, a company that made signs, and ordered a sign for the top of the Magnolia Building. Their logo had to rotate and also had to be seen all over Dallas. Magnolia placed the order in September and wanted it by November 8. This gigantic and almost impossible project was given to the treasurer and chief engineer of the company, Mr. J.B. McMath. Mr. McMath was not a schooled engineer, he was just smart. He had come to Dallas in 1917 and had done well with his mechanical abilities. Now, he had an almost unthinkable undertaking. Right off, Mr. McMath knew there had to be two horses with the mechanics stationed between them. The horses were made, 30 by 40 feet. Now, how was he going to make the monster turn? One evening Mr. McMath went to sleep, and in a dream the whole mechanical precept was given to him. He always claimed that God laid out the plans in that dream. In fact, this gentleman always gave God the credit for any of his accomplishments. Therefore, a giant wheel was made that would run on a circular track that could be electrically powered to make that horse go round and round. It worked!

The parts of the big Pegasus were taken up on the elevators of the building, and finally the horse was in place. All was ready but the lighting. The neon tubing was not on. Unfortunately, just when the tubing was ready to be placed, Texlite burned to the ground, so the tubing had to be reblown right up on top of the building itself. By November 7, 1934, the magnificent flying red horse was turned on. It rotated and it was seen all over Dallas. That horse turned until the 1970's when the electricity was turned off. Just a little power and Pegasus would start revolving again.

As a child I remember I could see that horse from my backyard only if my daddy would lift me up on his shoulders. This was a great thrill. On summer nights, I wouldn't go to bed until Daddy had boosted me up so that I could tell the Magnolia horse good night. Kind of corny—but true. We Dallas natives love Pegasus!

PAUL A. TOHMS PHOTO - DALLAS

Chapter 11

Periodical Documents and personal letter from the 1950's

Hudkins, Lonnie, One Miss—and Out, Sign Workers Get up in the World But Only Get to Make Lone Miscue, Dallas Morning News, 11 March 1952

Men like W.H.. Guernsay and R.C. Brown only get to make one mistake in their line of business and then they are through--permanently.

Their job consists of installing and repairing neon and metal tubing signs atop such edifices as the Magnolia and Mercantile National Bank buildings.

"You only have one close call in this type of business," said Mr. Guernsey as his steel grey eyes scanned the sidewalk 27 stories below, "and that's all."

The interview took place just below Dallas' famous Flying Red Horse sign perched above the Magnolia Building.

Mr. Guernsey, who stands 5 feet 5 inches and weighs a trim 130 pounds, has been an employee of Texlite, Inc., for 26 of his 40 years or ever since he came to Dallas from his native Albany, N.Y.

"I have been with the company so long," he said, "that I am the second number on the payroll."

He makes his home with his wife and four children at 4018 Pennsylvania Ave. "None of my children seem inclined to follow in my footsteps," he quipped.

Mr. Brown, who stands 5 feet 6 inches and weighs 130 pounds, has been in the business only five years. He's 34.

Before he came to Dallas, he served in Navy aviation ordinance during World War II and before that operated a café at Phoenix, Ariz. "The tallest building in Phoenix is a hotel," he recalled, "and the only thing really high about that establishment in the price of a room."

He and his wife and son live in a comfortable home he purchased at Irving under the GI Bill.

Both men have a reasonable amount of insurance—company insurance—but are reluctant to talk too much about the subject. "We are very careful," they pointed out.

For a real thrill, Mr. Guersney suggests working on the neon clock on the east side of the Mercantile Building. "It's a straight drop to the sidewalk," he explained.

Inasmuch as Texlite supplies all types of signs for its customers throughout the nation, the men are not confined only to the serial work on the ground.

"We don't mind the high work," Mr. Brown said, "but have less worries about longevity downstairs."

Actually, only one sign worker in the company's history has been injured while working and that was when he came in contact with a "hot" wire. He escaped with only a badly burned arm.

However, high voltage is always danger on such signs as the Flying Red Horse, which requires 15,000 volts. "The amps are low, though," explained Mr. Guersney.

One of the world's largest faced signs, architecturally integrated with an attractive modern building, and identifies First National Bank, Temple, Texas. Plastic portion of the sign, 130 feet in height, uses weather-resistant Plexiglas acrylic plastic. In this application, yellow translucent acrylic is employed to achieve even diffusion of light from more than 3,000 feet of colored neon tubing which lights both sign portion and 55-foot beacon above.

Each face of the sign is composed of corrugated Plexiglas panels 3/16 inches thick, approximately four feet wide and six feet high, with 2 and 1/2 in, corrugations running vertically. Four-foot high green letters of acrylic plastic contrast with yellow background, giving readability at long distances as well as pleasing color combinations by day or night. Entire sign structure weighs 18 tons, yet not visible cables or other supporting members disturb its symmetry. Huge sign was designed, fabricated and erected by McMath-Axilrod Corp., Dallas, in cooperation with Dallas architects. Plexiglas is product of Rohm & Haas, Philadephia.

J.B. and Mae McMath

This letter is a continuing example of J.B. Sr.'s Christian witness to those around him in all aspects of his life.

December 4, 1951

Mr. Frank L. Dow

Robstown, Texas

Dear Frank:

I have wanted to write you ever since I paid you a short visit, as I passed by on my recent trip to the Valley. If it had not been that my son-in-law and daughter were with me, I would have stayed longer and had a talk with you.

I did not even have a chance to tell you that I have been a Christian for some years since I have been away from Marlin. I am as positive of the existence of an Almighty God and His power and willingness to save a man's soul, as I am that I am living. There was a time that I didn't even believe the Bible. It was more or less a fairy story, as far as I was concerned. People who professed to be Christians—most of them—seemed to be no better than anyone else.

The Lord finally got hold of my heart and revealed to me beyond a shadow of a doubt that His word in the Bible was true from cover to cover. He gave me an understanding of the Scriptures that was amazing to me. Upon repenting of my sins and calling upon Him for mercy, He saved me, and He has been my guide in my business dealings and every movement of any consequence in my life for over thirty years. I do not mean that I have not made mistakes and had to ask God to forgive me many times, but I can certainly testify to the saving grace, the mercy, and the love of God.

I knew your precious father was a wonderful Christian, and not having had a chance to ask you, I am just wondering whether or not either of you boys have followed in his footsteps.

I have always thought a lot of you, Frank, not only because I have always found you ready to do the fair thing, but because you also remind me of your father so much. And while I have no grounds to question your spirituality, I, at the same time, would be happy to know whether or not you are serving the Lord. After all, the salvation of a man's soul is the most important business in the world, and He and God alone can take care of it.

I will be praying for you, Frank, and hope to hear from you at your convenience.

Sincerely,

J.B. McMath

Afterthought: Don't you just love this letter? It is such an example of how if you felt the Lord wanted you to say something to someone and for some reason or another it didn't get done, you can still address the subject with love and concern for the person at a later time. I hope that I never miss an opportunity for a divine appointment, but if I do, I want to remember I could try again with a letter like this one.

Chapter 12

Beginnings of Christ for the Nations and a New Age of the Outpouring of the Holy Spirit in the 1960's

Prelude: According to Wikipedia Christ for the Nations Institute is an educational arm of the ministry of Christ for the Nations, Inc., which was founded by Gordon and Freda Lindsey in July 1970. CFNI is an interdenominational charismatic Bible college located in Dallas, Texas. The organization has trained more than 33,000 students, reached 120 nations, and assisted native congregations in building more than 12,500 churches all over the world. The Lindsay's son, Dennis, is the current president of CFNI.

My association with Christ for the Nations by J.B. McMath, Sr.

I had known Brother Lindsay by sight, and from what I had heard and read about him for several years prior to his moving to Dallas in the early 1950's. However, I cannot recall the occasion or the date of our informal introduction, which occurred sometime after his arrival in Dallas.

Our first real get together was in the early 1960's when Brother Lindsay invited me to visit him at his office, at which time he informed me that he was in the process of forming a board of directors for his organization, and asked me if I would serve as a member.

Even though our association up to this time had been very limited, I nevertheless was impressed because of what I had learned about Brother Gordon Lindsay, and his reputation as a fruitful, dedicated man of God and I accepted the invitation as a great honor, and therefore became a member of his board, and am currently still a member after approximately 18 years.

This was the beginning of 18 years of some of the most profitable and enjoyable fellowship of my entire life. To be associated with such a fast growing, God fearing organization, led by a man and wife so dedicated to the will of God, has been an inspiration, only equalized by my own church where I have been attending for 30 years, Lakewood Memorial Assembly of God.

Footnote:I would like to mention some of the ways Christ for the Nations impacted the rest of the McMath family. As Granddaddy and Grandmother were the patriarch and matriarch of the family, we all followed their leadership in most things, and very closely when it came to all things spiritual. Sundays were always set aside for church and most of us went along with the grandparents to Lakewood Assembly of God Church. This belief is talked about in the Bible in Genesis 20:8 -10, which is the list of the Ten Commandments. It says, "Remember the Sabbath day (Sunday) to keep it holy. Six days shalt thou labour, and do all thy work. But the seventh day is the Sabbath of the Lord thy God: During it thou shall not do any work, thou, or thy son, nor thy daughter, thy manservant, nor thy maidservant, nor thy cattle, nor thy stranger that is within thy gates." This scripture means to keep Sunday holy by setting it apart as different from other days by ceasing one's labor in order to rest, serve God and concentrate on the things concerning eternity, spiritual life and God's honor. The Israelites were expected to model their conduct after God's work in creation. The Sabbath is a sign that we belong to God. After church we always went to lunch at Wyatt's Cafeteria, at Lakewood Shopping Center where the grandparents would graciously pay for lunch for all of us in the family and whomever we brought to church. In the case of my husband and I, it was a lot of starving hippie college students from the Jesus movement who were not just physically hungry but also hungry for more of God. After lunch, the grandparents would drive over to Oak Cliff for the Christ for the Nation service that started at 2:30. They really set aside the Sabbath for worship and rest and were faithful in attendance to both church and Christ for the Nations.

Another of my favorite memories of Christ for the Nations was the monthly ladies luncheons I would attend with grandmother. I don't think she ever missed one even though she rode the city bus to get there, as during this time she had given up driving (she was in her eighties).

The grandparent's house was always a safe haven for all the grandchildren. I especially remember coming and staying a week at a time in the summer so I could take my children to Bible school at Lakewood Assembly of God Church. You will read about Gordon Lindsay (the head of CFNI) as being a prolific writer who wrote about 250 books in his lifetime and I know that granddaddy owned all of them because they were scattered all over the house. The books were about interesting subjects from the Bible that you could never understand on your own and Gordon Lindsay would explain what they meant, like books entitled The Beast from the Bottomless Pit and Rise 666 of the Anti Christ. They were great reading when you were bored and could give you some nightmares! They could also scare you enough to keep you from sinning!

Of course, we had heard over and over that granddaddy had helped start Christ for the Nations with a donation, but I had always heard that the first building Christ for the Nations bought was a former bowling alley, not a bar. Maybe they didn't want to tell us it had started in a bar. I found an account of this story in a Christ for the Nations Magazine dated April 1981, written by Freda Lindsay and entitled This Generation's Shrewd:

Mrs. Lindsay says, I think of a breakfast meeting Gordon and I held in 1965 at the Alpine Club in Dallas. The building had been used for a nightclub. The owner had gone bankrupt; the sheriff had padlocked the doors. Now the building was up for sale, Gordon and I had prayed about it and felt God had plans for that place. So we received permission to use the club for a breakfast to which we invited a dozen or so Christian businessmen.

After eating, we shared our plans. Each person who spoke had only negative things to say: "The building is a white elephant." "It has gone bankrupt several times." "There is a curse on it." "It's the wrong location." "No one would invest $125,000 in this venture," etc. I saw Gordon's face drop—but not his spirit.

After the breakfast was over, an elderly retired gentleman, J.B. McMath, Sr., came quietly to Gordon and said, "If you feel this is God, then I'll give you $1,000.00 to put down on it."

And that encouragement was all Gordon needed. Shortly thereafter we purchased the nightclub and started Christ for the Nations. J.B. has watched the Institute grow from 50 to 1500 this year, what joy he radiates as he sits in some of the classes. Yes, he had been shrewd in his business investments. He was also wise in his spiritual stewardship. What a reward he will have!

May God help each one who reads these words to be wise, prudent and shrewd for the Lord in matters of finances.

Afterthought: This seems like a good time to talk about the Bible's teaching about money or, in the Biblical language, tithes and offerings. J.B.'s thoughts about tithing agreed with the Bible from Malachi (Old Testament) 3: 8,10, "Will a man rob God? Yet ye have robbed me. But ye say, wherein have we robbed thee? In tithes and offerings. Bring ye all the tithes into the storehouse, that there may be meat in thy house, and prove me now herewith, saith the Lord of hosts, If I will not open the windows of heaven, and pour you out a blessing, that there shall not be room to receive it." This passage means that if believers would begin to support their ministers with their tithes (10 per cent of their income) and offerings God would abundantly bless them. The blessings that accompany faithfulness in financial giving will come both in this life and the hereafter. At the heart of tithing is the notion that God owns everything. In addition to tithes, believers are encouraged to bring numerous offerings to the Lord. Believers are also encouraged to give freewill offerings. Tithing helps us not to be greedy for money. Our tithes are given to advance God's kingdom, especially the work of the local church, and to spread the gospel throughout the world and help those in need. Tithing should be voluntary and generous. We should be willing to give our tithes sacrificially because that is the way Jesus Christ gave his life to us. Our tithing should be done cheerfully because the Bible says in 2 Corinthians 9:7 that the Lord loves a cheerful giver. Looking back now and knowing that Christ for the Nations is still an active missionary school I cannot tell you how proud we the family are that Granddaddy contributed to that great school. The school is still fulfilling the great commission of Christ (Matthew 28:19) which says, "Go ye therefore, and teach all nations, baptizing them in the name of the Father, and of the Son, and of the Holy Ghost: teaching them to observe all things whatsoever I have commanded you, and lo, I am with you always, even unto the end of the world." Eternity will only know how many souls for Christ have been won through this thriving ministry. It is truly an eternal legacy that we are more proud of him for than any of his other accomplishments.

Additional Newspaper Article about Christ for the Nations

Bidell, Doug, Witnessing Pentecostals, the Dallas Morning News, 20 November 1986

In 1965, an unusual pair of potential buyers approached the owner of a padlocked and bankrupt Oak Cliff bar.

Pentecostal evangelists Freda and Gordon Lindsay wanted the 6,000 square foot Kiest Boulevard watering hole for—all things—a permanent lecture hall devoted to the pursuits of Charismatic Christianity.

For $125,000, the Alpine Night Club became the Dallas Christian Center and the face of Dallas at Interstate 35E and US Highway 67 was forever changed.

Today, 13 years after the death of Gordon Lindsay, the Godly enterprise nurtured by the couple encompasses 76 acres of prime property—including apartment complexes, a 2,500-seat auditorium and a $2.1 million tower that used to be the Oak Cliff Sheraton Inn.

More than 1,500 students of all religions swarm across the Christ for the Nation Institute each day on their way to classes in "witnessing," "practical sermoning," and "witnessing to children."

And, with 71-year old Freda Lindsay at the helm, the organization has spread worldwide via 17 foreign Bible schools and grants that have helped build more than 7,000 churches from Mexico to Mozambique.

"I don't know that we ever had one page of planning to all this," says Mrs. Lindsay. "To think that an organization could have grown this much with out any plan, it's just hard to believe."

"But all we have ever done is pray and say, "God, what next?"

The phenomenal expansion of Christ for the Nations is in large measure, a product of Gordon Lindsay's early work as a chronicler of charismatic crusades. During the 1930's, he was one of a handful of so-called "holy roller" evangelists who preached of spiritual healing and divine gifts to small-town churches and in tents floored with sawdust. Mrs. Lindsay, one of 12 children born to European immigrants on a Canadian homestead, was Gordon's behind the scenes business administrator during those first "sawdust trail" campaigns.

And they were tough years. On most nights the offerings gathered by the Lindsay's barely paid for the gasoline needed to make it to the next stop. On top of that, Pentecostal preachers were roundly ridiculed by even the most conservative established religions. The notion that the Holy Spirit could cure illnesses and provoke worshippers to talk in strange "tongues" was considered heresy.

Slowly however, the ministries of young Lindsay, Oral Roberts, Rex Humbard, Jack Coe, Kenneth Hagin, and other young preachers began gaining fury. And in 1947 while the Lindsay's were based in Shreveport, Louisiana Gordon decided to establish a sort of newsletter that would keep followers abreast of their favorite campaign's latest accomplishments.

He named it The Voice of Healing, and it was an overnight success. In the first five years of publication, its circulation topped 100,000. Meanwhile, Lindsay was writing the first of more than 250 books he would complete during his lifetime.

The enterprise soon outgrew printing and postal service capabilities of Shreveport, forcing the Lindsay's to find a new home. And in 1953, they settled in Dallas.

Inside a small headquarters building near the Alpine Night Club, the couple continued publishing the Voice of Healing, although the magazine's importance to the Lindsay's work soon dwindled.

"Gordon was in constant demand as a speaker," says Mrs. Lindsay. "He was an excellent writer, but he also had a superb teaching ability."

Lindsay's tours of primitive nations convicted him that missionary work in those countries should be brought to the forefront of his ministry. He began offering $250 construction grants to Third World evangelists, who applied in droves.

By 1965, Lindsay's missionary work, books and lectures had developed a devout following. When the Alpine building opened, the organization moved in and remodeled. Christ for the Nations Institute then opened its doors for the first 50 Bible students who were instructed by a staff of three.

Enrollment steadily increased, and so did the need for student housing. The institute bought seven adjacent apartment complexes, and then set about raising money for construction of a large new institute headquarters.

All seemed to be going well until April 1, 1973.

That day Gordon died as he sat on the auditorium stage listening to Mrs. Lindsay leading the school's 250 students in song.

"I never wanted the number one role, nor did I ever anticipate I would have to take over," says Mrs. Lindsay. "Then, overnight, I'm the editor of a magazine with Gordon's name on it. I mean, "Who's Freda?" people were asking. I'd really always stayed in the background while he was alive. And I'd never really written anything except through my diary and some minor chapters in Gordon's books."

At that point, Mrs. Lindsay and the institute faced immense debt. The seven apartment complexes weren't paying for themselves through student enrollment. In addition, three more years of payments were necessary to meet construction expenses for the new headquarters building.

I thought, "How in the world were we going to remain solvent?" Mrs. Lindsay recalls. "The first of every month we were scrounging just to get enough money to pay the mortgages on the seven dormitories."

But Mrs. Lindsay managed. Enrollment continued to climb. Several large cash donations were pledged to the institute. And benevolent benefactors, some of who barely knew of the organization's work, gave parcels of land up to 41 acres in size, some of which were sold to retire massive hunks of indebtedness or enlarge the campus.

With the backing of business manager Norman Young, a former bank executive, the widow pushed on with the institute's expansion. And it soon became apparent that the future of the school depended on more student funding.

"Attendance fluctuates on the basis of available housing," says Mrs. Lindsay's son Dennis. recently named president of the organization. "The more housing we have, the more students we have, it's just that simple."

The Bible school's students knew that. They began praying and fasting in hopes that the Sheraton Inn situated on a wedge of land at the "Y" of I-35 and US 87 soon would become theirs.

On occasion, groups of students would band together to perform a "Jericho march" around the monolithic white tower, claiming the structure for the institute and the Lord's work.

"I wondered if one to many Jericho marches might not prompt the manager to order them off the premises," Mrs. Lindsay wrote in her book, entitled Freda. "But so far as I know, he didn't. One day I heard that the hotel had been sold to a wealthy Muslim. The owner's son was most congenial, and we soon became friends."

In 1963, the institute hit upon a financing deal that proved acceptable to the Muslim owner of the Sheraton, and the Gordon Lindsay Tower was claimed for the institute's ministry.

With its giant red, white and blue lights and lettering on each side, the building today serves as both a dormitory and a billboard. "People see it all the time and come in and say, "What is this all about in here?" says Mrs. Lindsay. They go, "Are you a cult or something?"

But, more than anything, the high-rise building symbolizes Mrs. Lindsay's victory over adversity. "I had a friend who came to me not too long ago and said, "Everyone knew it would grow, but, he said now to see the work grow more rapidly with Gordon gone, it gives God even more glory. Everybody knows that a woman couldn't have done it."

"And I told him, "You're right, Especially this woman…I don't have that much going for me."

Christ for the Nations Institute owes it all to the prayer and faith of Gordon Lindsay, she says.

And the progress of the ministry shows no sign of slowing.

The school's 1,500 students – whose basic tuition begins at $525 per semester—come from all over the world. accepting scholarships and working odd jobs on campus to make their way through classes, then return to their native lands to set up ministries of their own. Another 100 students attend a branch school in New York.

And wherever they are, those enrolled in Christ for the Nations are required to spread their message daily through contacts on street corners, in bars, jails…even red-light districts.

Mrs. Lindsay says she will soon turn over much of the responsibilities for day-to-day administration of operations to a new leader.

The woman the students call "Mom" spends her days now either writing in her on-campus apartment or meeting with ex-students and missionaries who constantly line up at her office door to report on their own ministry's progress, many of which were backed with more than $2.3 million given away to the institute last year.

As her 72nd birthday approaches in April, Mrs. Lindsay says she is still striving to meet two goals. First, she wants to clear the Institute of all remaining building debts, which total about $500,000. "I want to leave it for the next person so he won't have to work as hard as I did," she says.

The second goal is one she and her husband set decades before.

"As long as one man or woman, one boy or girl, lives without Christ, then our job is not finished."

Freda Lindsay and Mae McMath

Chapter 13

Additional Newspaper Articles from the 1960's, Prayer and Another Dream

Altwegg, Al, Milestones for a Landmark. Dallas Morning News, 23 June 1962

There will be no cake with 40 candles, but this week marks the birthday of a Dallas landmark which was the tallest building in Dallas for 20 years, the Mobil Building (formerly the Magnolia Building) in the heart of downtown Dallas.

It was on June 22 in 1922 that the first offices were occupied in the structure, which at that time was surpassed in height by only two U.S. buildings outside New York City—the Travelers Insurance Building in Hartford and the L.C. Smith building in Seattle.

"When I designed that wonderful building, it was the tallest thing that had ever been built south of Washington, D.C., even by the Aztecs," said the building's architect, Sir Alfred Charles Bossom, a Conservative member of the British Parliament as well as a world-renowned architect.

More than 400 feet tall, the 27-story building towered over the Dallas skyline, and the Magnolia Petroleum Co.'s offices took up only six floors of its 176,750 square feet of office space.

Today, the Socony Mobil Oil Co.'s offices fill the entire building except for the first floor. It is the headquarters for a wide variety of Mobil operations employing almost 2,000 persons in Dallas County.

Back in 1958, Socony Mobil (which had taken over Magnolia) was having troubles. And in that year President Albert L. Nickerson, a tough-minded administrator, took over as chief executive officer and proceeded to "trim the fat" out of the Socony Mobil operation.

Dallas was hit, along with the rest of the nation, in a major reorganization, and the word ran through town that Socony Mobil (or Magnolia) that people were moving to other parts of the country left and right.

Now that the dust has settled, however, it appears that Dallas did not lose so much. Where the worldwide company trimmed down from 77,500 employees in 1957 to 63,700 last year (almost 18 per cent) the Dallas employment of the company dropped from about 2,200 to a little under 2,000 today. (or 10 per cent).

Mobil today is not only the largest oil company in Dallas in terms of employment, but it is one of the top 10 industrial employers in the country.

The Dallas Mobil Building is now headquarters for:

1. The Southwest Marketing Division, which handles all marketing in Texas, Louisiana, Oklahoma, New Mexico, and Arkansas. In that area, more than 5,000 retail outlets will sell more than 650 million gallons of petroleum products in 1962.

2. Magnolia Pipe Line Co., one of the nation's largest, with 13,000 miles of pipelines in 21 states.

3. Dallas Accounting and Service Center, the largest of five in the U.S. in number of persons employed and scope of work handled. It issues some 40,000 checks monthly for royalty and working interest in oil and gas production, pays bills, and issues all payroll checks for Mobil's exploration and producing divisions east of the Rockies. It handles payroll for about 8,000 persons and each week pays more than 10,000 invoices. Each month it keypunches some 750,000 data processing cards, enough to make a pile the height of the Mobil Building.

Dallas is also headquarters for Mobil's Field Research Laboratory, one of the five the company has, with more than 75 men here holding Ph.D. degrees. The installation consists of 35 buildings on 140 acres of land.

Also here is the Geophysical Services Group, which supervises Mobil's geophysical crews all over the U.S. and assists in some of the company's foreign geophysical operations, gathering scientific data on the earth's sub-surface in the search for oil.

Still one of the most conspicuous signs on the Dallas horizon is the Flying Red Horse, which was placed atop the Mobil Building in 1934.

That shining light in the Dallas night consists of two Pegasus figures of neon, mounted 14 feet apart, each horse 30 feet high and 40 feet long. The sign weighs 7,000 pounds.

And as it rotates over Dallas, there are still people who chuckle at the old gag, probably dreamed up by someone from Houston or Fort Worth, that the sign was made of two horses to keep Dallas from being a "one-horse" town.

Dallas is far from a one-horse town in the Socony Mobil scheme of things.

1966: A Five Year Prayer Meeting, and a Great Lesson it Taught Me by J.B. McMath, Sr.

A group of men, all members of The Dallas Chapter of the Full Gospel Businessmen, including myself, felt led in early 1966 to form a prayer group, to convene every Saturday morning at 6:30 a.m. Realizing that Christ for the Nations Christian Center had one of the best facilities in the city for a group prayer meeting, we decided to contact Brother Gordon Lindsay for permission to use their prayer room, and it seemed to delight his heart to say yes, you are more than welcome, for we are always happy and anxious to encourage and promote prayer anywhere and at any time. We used this prayer room freely for over five years. This was one of the finest facilities to pray in that I have ever experienced, not only because of its fine accommodations but because it was located in a place that always had the covering power of the Holy Spirit.

To make the prayer meeting just as flexible and convenient as possible, it was decided that everyone be present at as near 6:30 a.m. as possible, and pray just as long as they felt led to do so. Some of our men worked

Saturday mornings and had to leave in time to be on the job by work time, consequently anyone was free to leave as the occasion required. The prayer meeting always lasted a minimum of one hour and many times much longer, as we felt led to pray.

The prime purpose for the prayer meeting was to pray for God's Spirit and anointing in our lives and for it to be more abundantly present in our weekly meetings, and that we would continue to be a growing and fruitful organization until Jesus returns.

However, for our particular purpose the meeting place had one great handicap; it was in South Oak Cliff, and by far the great majority of our men lived in North and East Dallas, therefore the driving distance to and from the prayer meeting was the prime handicap of our attendance.

We had as I can recall about fifteen men at our first meeting, and the average for the next four to six weeks ran between ten and fifteen.

After that, we had a real decline in numbers. There were only four men who didn't come all at the same time because their work wouldn't permit it. I got discouraged and prayed and told the Lord that as long as their was me and two other men coming, I would not stop going. It went along for months and two men and myself would always show up.

And then finally for two Saturdays in succession we had just one brother and myself present, and on the second Saturday this occurred I prayed and reminded the Lord that I promised to attend as long as there were two present besides me. The next Saturday morning, when I stopped at the signal light where the exit intercepts with Kiest Boulevard, just one block from the prayer meeting, the Lord spoke to me in a very firm but inaudible voice, and said, "For where two or three are gathered together in my name, there I am in the midst of them." Matthew 18:20. This, of course, was a very familiar scripture, but far more meaningful this morning than ever before.

I knew beyond the least shadow of a doubt that the Lord was very definitely speaking to me, and telling me that a crowd was no prerequisite for an effective prayer meeting, that all we needed was Jesus and he had promised to always be present where two or three were gathered together in his name.

As soon as I realized the Lord had spoken to me, I replied, "Lord, I will continue attending this prayer meeting just as long as there is one present besides me.

However, not long afterwards we again had only one present for two meetings in succession, and I decided to pray about it again; I said, "Lord, I promised to continue attending this prayer meeting just as long as there was one present besides myself and now for two successive mornings we have had only one beside me, now what about that?"

I had no more than gotten the words out of my mouth when the Lord answered me and said, "I said where two or three," and I replied immediately, "Lord I will continue attending this prayer meeting just as long as there is one present besides me."

At this time, which was 1970, I was nearing my 76th birthday, and had always had a longing to visit the holy lands, and knew at my age the longer I put it off the less likely I would ever make the trip.

Christ for the Nations had a trip scheduled for June 5th through the 20th of that year, and I decided to go with them. This would, of course, force me to miss three of our prayer meetings, something I had to do with a certain amount of reluctance. However, my knowing this could be my last opportunity to make such a trip outweighed all mental reservations to the contrary, and I went.

My wife had made the same tour two years previously, and at a time when I did not feel led to go, and the first thing she said to me on her return was, "I am surely glad you didn't go, for at your age you would not have been physically able to do all the walking and climbing we had to do."

Now, being two years older and definitely planning to make this trip, according to my dear wife when I told her that I was definitely going and trusting God to take care of me she gave me some good advice and told me that if I would follow it religiously, I might make it. Here was her advice: If you do not feel like getting up in the morning, just stay in bed and rest, and let the others go without you. If you are on the bus and do not feel like getting off and walking with the others, just stay on the bus and rest. If you will adhere to these two rules, you might make it.

Approximately ten other Dallasites made the tour with us, and I offer any one of them as a witness, that I was in their midst wherever they went, and that was not at the tail end of the line either.

We were to return to our hotel in the afternoon or evening, and eat a hearty meal, and one or more of the men and myself would go window shopping or sightseeing until bed time, and get up the next morning, eat breakfast and repeat the same routine every day, and never once did I experience a single moment's fatigue.

My wife met our plane when we arrived back in Dallas on Saturday evening the 20th and I felt as fresh and as relaxed as I did the day I boarded the plane for the tour.

As far as my physical being was concerned I do not believe I had ever experienced a greater miracle, and to our precious Lord be many thanks and all the glory. I believe those few men of the prayer group prayed for me during my absence and the Lord greatly blessed me with a wonderful trip.

Our plane arrived home on Saturday evening just one week before our next prayer meeting, and I awoke at the proper time as usual to make the meeting on time.

Four weeks had passed since I had attended an early morning prayer meeting, and no doubt I was just a little spoiled for when I awoke, I just turned over in the bed and remarked to myself, "Wouldn't it be wonderful if I could just remain in bed another hour or two"; and then I asked the Lord about the most selfish question anyone could have asked, one I am ashamed to have to mention. I asked the Lord, "What am I getting out of this prayer meeting anyhow?" If I had asked him what am I contributing to the meeting he would no doubt have answered me much differently, but he just answered with one word: "Exercise." His voice though inaudible was so real and forceful that I rolled out of bed like I was going to a fire and went to the prayer meeting. I assume the word "exercise," meant he hadn't released me to not pray during this time even if there was only one brother joining me in prayer.

Not long after this our regular attendance dropped to just two, and remained at that number until the middle of 1971 after which my other Christian brother and myself had a brief discussion one morning following our prayer meeting.

I remarked to him, that if people came to the meeting just because we persuaded or begged them, that they would make little if any contribution thereto, for the simple reason that their heart would not be in it, and I suggested that we just leave the matter in the hands of the Lord and let him work it out in his own will, and for his own glory.

To this suggestion my Christian brother heartily agreed and added, "Let's just pray that God himself will speak to our Full Gospel Chapter and inspire someone to start a prayer meeting that more will participate in."

Evidently our prayers were answered, for no more than two weeks following our resolution and prayer, another Christian brother, then president of our Dallas Chapter, announced a prayer meeting to convene at the Statler Hilton Hotel every Monday night to pray for the success of the convention.

Even though the prayer meeting was supposed to close with the convention we nevertheless felt so sure that it was an answer to prayer that we closed our prayer meeting, after over five years, and joined with the Dallas Chapter, and the prayer meeting is still convening with good attendance after three years.

Until this time the financing of our conventions were sometimes a problem. I can remember one year when we lacked some $2500.00 meeting expenses and the directors and a few members had to make up the difference. However, the three conventions, which have followed the calling of this prayer meeting, have been three of our best and each one closed with a surplus above expenses.

It was the consensus that the prayer meeting was a great contributing factor in the conventions great success and for that reason it was decided to continue it indefinitely.

I wish to make it clear that we have never prayed for a surplus from our conventions, but for a good convention, and that all expenses be met, for the glory of God.

The words the Lord no doubt spoke to me on at least three occasions during our five year prayer meeting, and particularly the word "exercise" which was the final word spoken have inspired me to write the account of the experience, and to also include some of my very own personal views concerning prayer and its great importance according to the scriptures.

More on prayer by J.B:

Naturally, as every parent should, I have consistently prayed for my children from their birth, with the faith and hope that not one would be lost, but that each one would be genuinely converted to the Lord Jesus Christ, at an early age.

As they grew older, I prayed more earnestly that God would give to each of them some outstanding salvation experience that would be a stabilizing influence in their Christian lives and keep them from falling away, when trials and tribulations come upon them, as they do to all Christians.

I continued praying this prayer until the Lord finally spoke to my heart one evening and asked me, what is the most outstanding experience in your Christian life? and I was instantly reminded of what happened to me the first morning following my conversion in the latter part of April 1916, when the Spirit of God revealed to my heart the truth and the infallibility of God's eternal word, the Bible.

The lesson the Lord was trying to teach me, was, if I wanted my children to be able to stand when the world is on fire, then give them God's word. This also goes for the old as well as the young. The word of God is the most secure anchor for the soul under all adverse circumstances, than can befall mortal man.

Psalm 119:105 says, "Thy word is a lamp unto my feet, and a light unto my path. (It is the only book I know, that tells me from whence I came, and to whither I go.)

Afterthought: This story reminds me of the story in Mark 14. When Jesus knew he was about to be arrested and taken to be crucified he knew he should spend some time in prayer. And he went to a garden area called Gethsemane with his disciples and this is what happened according to The Message Bible: When Jesus had prayed he came back to his disciples and found them asleep. He said to Peter, "Simon, you went to sleep on me? Can't you stick it out with me in prayer for just one hour? Stay alert, be in prayer, so you don't enter the danger zone without even knowing it. Don't be naïve. Part of you is eager, ready for anything in God; but another part is as lazy as an old dog sleeping by the fire."

Jesus went back and prayed again. Returning, he again found them sound asleep. They simply couldn't keep their eyes open, and they didn't have a plausible excuse.

He came back a third time and said, "Are you going to sleep all night? No—you've slept long enough. Time's up."

Jesus wants us to have conversation with him daily in prayer and tell him our needs and pray for others. Stay alert to pray and don't roll over and go back to sleep.

J. B.'s statement at the beginning of this section turned out to be prophetic. His son, Edward, as a young boy came to know the Lord and wanted to be baptized. J.B. and Mae were hesitant because of his age but finally allowed him to be baptized. The next week he was running across the street near his home when a car struck and killed him. J.B. and Mae were comforted by his public confession of Jesus Christ at such an early age.

Lakewood Church Dream written by J.B. McMath

Prelude: It occurs to me that some of you who will be reading this book will have little or no background in what the Bible says or what it means.

This gives me the pleasure of revealing some of the words and ideas that are in the Bible and explaining them. In this particular story of J.B. Sr.'s he tells of a supernatural dream that he had. It lines up with scripture from Acts 2:17 which says, "And it shall come to pass in the last days, saith God, I will pour out my Spirit upon all flesh, and your sons and your daughters shall prophesy, and your young men shall see visions, and your old men shall dream dreams." J.B. certainly qualified as an old man at this time and he had a dream in which the Spirit of God told him what would be brought forth from his church in the future.

This dream was given to J.B. McMath Sr. in the spring of 1968 concerning Lakewood Memorial Assembly of God Church in Dallas, Texas (this church still exists today).

I feel like I should include a couple of things that happened prior to this dream that show you how invested J.B. and Mae McMath were in Lakewood Church. When they moved to the area of Lakewood, down the street from the Lakewood Country Club grandmother began to tell J.B. that they needed a Pentecostal church in the neighborhood. J.B. told Mae that it would never happen, that there would never be a Pentecostal church in the prominent neighborhood of Lakewood. Grandmother was not discouraged by his comments but began to scour the neighborhood to find a lot to build a church on. When she found one, she began to drive there every day and pray, and claim the lot for the Lord. From the Biblical account, she would do a Jericho march around the land to claim it for the Lord's use. In the Old Testament book of Joshua, chapters 1-6 is the story about how the Israelites conquered Jericho. God told Joshua and his soldiers to march around the walls of Jericho once each day carrying the Ark of the Covenant, and to be quiet while they were marching. Then, on the seventh day they marched around the walls seven times, then the soldiers shouted, and all the walls of the city fell flat and the Israelites went in and conquered the city. People today still do Jericho marches around places they want to conquer for the Lord. I don't know how long Mae was led to do this but I do know that the end result was that the lot was bought for a church and Lakewood Memorial was built there.

After the church was built, it was J.B. McMath, Sr. that hired Brother Fjordbak to take the role of preacher for the church.

The dream is as follows from J.B. Srs.' own words: It was time for the evening services, and I was sitting in the east row of seats about 3 or 4 pews from the front entrance and every seat in the church was occupied.

There was nothing unusual or different about the church unless it was that while every available seat was taken, there was not a single person requiring a chair in the isle as is so often needed under similar circumstances.

Suddenly the Pastor arose from among the congregation, several seats back from the altar, in the center section, and made his way to the platform or pulpit where he picked up a trumpet resting on a chair between the pulpit and the piano, and began playing the most beautiful soul stirring melody I had ever heard.

After playing for about 60 seconds before the congregation, he marched off the platform and out the east side door, and down the outside of the church to the front walk, and then back to the same door from which he exited, playing the same melody as he marched, but stopped playing as he re-entered the church.

I certainly am not a musician, but I do have an ear and a great love for good, especially sacred music, and I could discern that it was a most difficult composition, and that his performance or rendition was perfect.

While marching and playing he began speaking what appeared to be the words to the song through the trumpet, and without in any way effecting the perfect continuity or a single note of the melody.

You could understand that the words were spoken very distinctly and in English. However upon awakening I could not remember a single word that was spoken or the melody.

In my dream I turned to the man sitting next to me and remarked to him, "Isn't that wonderful?" and he replied, "Yes, it is wonderful."

The volume seemed to be as great as if several trumpets were playing at the same time, and in perfect accord, and you got this feeling that the music was echoing like rays of light throughout the heavens and over a wide range of the church area.

As before stated the pastor stopped playing as he re-entered the church, and at that instant the entire congregation arose to their feet in perfect unison as one man and I began to weep, and I wept with them with the same feelings and emotions as if I had been awake.

We did not weep because we were sad but because the sweet presence of the Lord was so real that it brought a sacred reverence, and a mellowing to the heart of everyone present.

This dream was so vivid, and real, so orderly, and given with such precision, and with such sacred feelings that I cannot but believe it was God given, and since so much and so many are involved, I feel it was for the benefit of the church as a whole, and not for me alone.

I feel the implications are very plain and do not need a lot of theorizing or assuming, which many times confuses and conceals the real meaning. Therefore I will be brief and to the point in what I believe the interpretation to be.

Brother Fjdrobak's part in the dream should be accepted to mean that he is God's minister for the church.

His marching off the platform, and out the east door of the church, and down to the front walk and back while playing with such great volume, should be accepted to mean that his ministry and the ministry of this church is not to be confined to its own congregation and four walls alone. The great volume of the trumpet indicates, its bounds and responsibilities are limitless.

When he re-entered the church everyone arose to their feet in perfect unison. The explanation for this is very simple. Everyone is well aware of the great unity that prevails in our church, and that is what this act indicated, "perfect unity."

The weeping that followed resulting from the presence of the Lord being so real means that he is in our midst, and that He is ready to give us a great revival if we will pray, and stay humble, and mellow before him.

Afterthought: There were two articles written about Pastor Fjordbak and Lakewood Assembly of God Church that appeared in D Magazine. The first is entitled The Faith Healers by Bill Porterfield from October 1977. I would like to quote from the first article to validate the prophetic dream:

Fjordbak's church on Abrams Road has not only grown in congregation and capital, it also has brought together people who were once separated by boundaries of class and denomination. Protestants of every stripe mix with Roman Catholics and Jews. A vice-president of Coca-Cola and a vice-president of Dr. Pepper prayed at the altar last week. A Jew, the son of a Centennial Liquor Stores executive, is in charge of the children's school. A Catholic craftsman made the marvelous windows of colored glass; a Methodist designed the pastor's study. A Baptist built cabinets and a Church of Christ man was the contractor. All have taken up the Pentecostal creed.

Fjordbak has taken to establishing himself with other pastors who have aligned themselves with Pentecostal doctrine such as Paul Morrell of Tyler Street Methodist Church, Howard Conatser of Beverly Hills Baptist, Bobbie Cavnar, Catholic of the Children of God's Delight, and Ted Nelson of the Episcopal Church of the Resurrection. Fjordbak is doubtless the leader of this new band of Pentecostals—they all speak of him with admiration. And it was he who brought them together for the first time on a Pentecost Sunday three years ago. Now they meet once a month. "We eat together, pray together and counsel one another," Fjordbak says. "It is the finest fellowship of my life."

I would now like to quote for you a portion of the second article from The Dallas Morning News Dallas Life Magazine from August 28, 1983 entitled The New Fundamentalists by Sheila Taylor that also verifies the prophetic dream:

Pastor E.M. Fjordbak of the Lakewood Assembly of God agrees that a trend toward fundamentalism exists in the church today, and he has thirty years' experience to back his views. "This return is quite typical across the U.S.," he says. "In the past, pastors were quite discouraged because no matter what we did, it was wrong. We could have stood on our heads and turned purple, and the young people would have said it was the wrong shade of purple."

The turnaround started with the teenagers of the early Seventies, he believes, and has developed to the point where now, the young people of the Eighties are the complete opposite of those of the Sixties.

"There are two classes of them today, good and bad, and you don't see the gray areas you saw in the Sixties, when kids revolted against everything. The kids of the Seventies are now professional people, and they're trying to find their way. They're taking another look at their lives and at God."

Fjordbak believes that fundamentalism's strong doctrine attracts rather than repels these young people. "We have strong requirements at our church, and that's what they're looking for. They want strong commitments. They no longer have a cocky attitude. My own opinion is that some churches have been too liberal and took a "We'll let this pass," attitude. But young people want strong guidelines, so I set them, and they love me. We drill into people, "Yes, you can make something of yourself."

His church's Wednesday night prayer meetings attract about 300 in the 20 to 35 age group, and his 1,400 membership represents former members from 25 denominations: forty percent Roman Catholic, ten percent Church of Christ, and the rest everything from Methodist to former cult members. "We have wealthy and poor, black, Mexican and white, educated and uneducated, and it works beautifully. People with money are coming back because money wasn't happiness. Quite a few are coming back for a simple walk with God. After thirty years, I'm still excited. We're beginning to feel good again."

Pastor Fjordbak died on August 20, 2008 at the age of 87. I feel I should offer some of the details from his obituary that confirm the validity of the dream:

Fjordbak established Lakewood Productions, a television and video studio, which produced teaching tapes for churches and home Bible study groups across the nation. He felt called not to build buildings or a religious empire, but to be a shepherd to those willing to be led to the Lord. Reaching out to people from all walks of life, his diverse church was the subject of a nationally aired review by the TV program 60 Minutes and by local publications such as D Magazine and Texas Monthly.

Afterthought: Not only was Pastor Fjordbak available to his congregation, other denominations, and the world at large, he was also available to my family. When my husband, at twenty years old wanted to receive the baptism of the Holy Spirit, he met with Pastor Fjordbak and the result was not only that my husband Charley spoke in tongues but both he and Pastor Fjordbak ended up on the floor so entrenched in the Holy Spirit that they both were laughing with joy. When my husband and I continued on in college and had a large prayer group and ministry among the hippies of the time, Pastor Fjordbak allowed us to bring students to him for prayer who needed more help than we knew how to give. We worked with special needs children in our jobs and he would meet with us and minister to them. When we had children, he dedicated all of our three daughters to the Lord soon after they were born. He certainly had fulfilled the dream that J.B. Sr. dreamed about him and his precious church, Lakewood Memorial Assembly of God. May we all fulfill the life and destinies the Lord has for each of us as his children. Are you working on yours?

Chapter 14

Personal Healing of 1976 by J.B. McMath, Sr. and Articles from the 1970's

I was seized in March 1976 with pain in my right leg from hip to ankle. The attack was so mild at first that I did not as much as make a mental note as the day of the month it occurred. However, it grew progressively worse for nine months, until I could get into no position in bed that would allow me to sleep without a sedative, and then the sedative would loose its effectiveness before the night ended, and I would have to either repeat the dosage, or get out of bed and sit in a chair, which was the only way I could rest without the sedative, and as a result I spent hours sleeping in a chair.

My pain worsened until I could not stand on my feet for any length of time without suffering excruciating pain. My wife and I attended our church Sunday morning November 28th, and our pastor, as is his custom, has the congregation stand for the reading of his text and prayer, the time for which seldom exceeds five minutes; but this morning my pain was so severe that it took all the willpower I could muster to refrain from sitting down before prayer was concluded.

We had also planned to attend the 2:30 afternoon service at Christ for the Nations, but my pain was so severe that I told my wife I did not feel like going, and she suggested we get something to eat, after which I might feel better. So we went to the cafeteria, and I could not even stand in the service line. Therefore we went home, and we went nowhere the following Sunday.

My daughter Rebecca called me every week, and sometimes several times during the week, to try to persuade me to see a doctor about my pain. The last time she called was Wednesday, December 8th, and I became just a little irritated with her persistence, and finally told her that God made me and knew all about me, and certainly could heal me, and that I was going to trust him for my healing. And she replied, "What if you die?" And I answered, "Well, I have but one time to die and if I have to die that will be all right also." Hebrews 9:27 says, "It is appointed once for man to die and then his judgment."

On Sunday, December 12th, just four days following this conversation with my daughter, my wife drove me to Christ for the Nations for the 2:30 afternoon services, following which I was to attend a board meeting scheduled to convene immediately following the service, and to save me of as much walking as possible, my wife put me out at the front of the auditorium, where I took a back seat near the entrance to await her return from parking the car.

Upon her return we moved several seats forward, and sat down, and we were no more than seated when the song leader approached the platform and asked everyone to stand for the singing of some choruses, and without thinking I stood to my feet and participated in the singing, which lasted at least twenty minutes. When I sat down I discovered that I had been instantly and completely healed of my pain and could not recall a single pain or discomfort during my standing while singing.

Grove, Larry. "Controversy in Dallas: A 'sign' of Character. Dallas Morning News.

Dallas may soon sign the death warrant for its thousands of signs—except for those nostalgic items that are "the character of the city."

But the decision of what is and what is not "character" has been the source of a boiling controversy that preceded the drafting of a new sign ordinance by the City Council in April.

When the ordinance is adopted, Dallas will have the most thoroughly researched sign measure ever adopted by the American city, said Dr. Bryghte Godbold, chairman of a 15-member committee that prepared recommendations on the ordinance for the Plan Commission.

It may also have the most thoroughly court-tested ordinance in existence.

Three companies who contend Dallas already has the power to regulate signs—a power that is not being used, have filed a suit in 193rd District Court.

Waldrum Sign Co., J.F. Zimmerman & Sons Inc. and Federal Sign and Signal Corp. claim in the suit that "business firms, large and small, are being penalized, restricted and discriminated against" by the proposed new ordinance.

No hearing date has as yet been set in the case.

Apparently 100 per cent safe are the signs that "mean something" to the character of the city. In short, the signs that have, by their familiarity, become definite features in the city's appearance.

The first sign that comes to mind is the Pegasus—the "Flying Red Horse"—atop the Mobil Building. Another is the John Carleton Mead—designed waterfall that used to tout Pearl-beer and now reminds us to smoke. Still another is the Sears sign on the old Lamar Street plant. And someone else called in to regret any dire possibilities of losing the Greyhound sign downtown, or the Fox that lopes alongside Stemmons Expressway for a photo processing company.

And the sign atop the building that once housed the Texas School Book Depository, says Godbold, would surely qualify as a landmark to be undisturbed until and unless owners want to remove it themselves.

Judging from calls to the Times Herald, the No. 1 favorite sign is the Flying Red Horse. "Don't let them take it down," said a gentle-voiced woman who said it has a special place in her memories.

"When it was first put up, my fiancée lived in Waco. He would tell me how eagerly he watched for the sign to come into view as he approached Dallas from the south.

"I should have married that young man," the lady said.

The sign was erected on the former Magnolia building in 1934, atop a 50-foot steel tower. The sign, more than 400 feet above street level, was the highest point of the skyline until the Mercantile Bank poked skyward at the close of World War II.

Actually, there are two horses up there, 30 feet high and 14 feet apart. At the time they were erected, it was evidence Dallas never again could be called a one-horse town.

It is not surprising the sign holds personal memories for residents who, for reasons of their own, hold a special fondness for Dallas.

One couple, not many years ago, was viewed holding noontime trysts under the mass of steel angles and neon tubing of the sign. Viewed from the nearby Lancers Club, and duly noted in the newspaper, the couple was seen there no more. But the story did not end there.

Some months later, the Lancers Club received an invitation for members to come en masse to a wedding. The couple good-naturedly acknowledged that noontime diners had shared in their courtship—so they might as well come to the wedding.

Mae and J.B. McMath, Sr.

Steeley, Jim. "Horse of a Different Color." Texas Highways Magazine," October 1981, pgs. 12-14.

Prelude: While getting permission to re-print this article from Mr. Steeley he sent this quote about J.B. and Mae:

"I was free lancing when I did the Texas Highways story on J.B. McMath. He was a gentle character and had been a part of significant Dallas history. I remember bowing for a prayer that he and his wife offered when we returned to their house after the photo adventure…so I'm not surprised that the daughter in law's book will have a historical and spiritual account of his life."

Eighty-six-year-old J.B. McMath's voice hints of breaking when he reverently refers to "my friend." His eyes water a bit, too. But when his narrative gains the momentum of hundreds of previous recitings, he closes his eyes and clips off precise figures of size, weight, age, and construction of this friend he seems to know so well.

Dallas's landmark, the "Flying Red Horse," has had many friends and supporters during its prolonged flight over Texas' second largest city, but none other as close or as intimate as McMath. His sign company designed and erected the aerial steed atop the downtown Magnolia Building in 1934. McMath supervised the job every step of the way. For 28 years, "Mr. Mac" and company maintained the 30 by 40 foot sign, which undoubtedly was Dallas' most prominent symbol until taller buildings surrounded it.

The R.L. Thornton Freeway supplanted the sign plant and its huge porcelain firing oven in 1962, and the company moved to McGregor. McMath soon retired and returned to Dallas near his friend.

The Flying Red Horse is obviously modeled on the theme of Pegasus, the winged horse of Greek mythology. As the legend goes, the noble Pegasus cut off the head of Medusa, that claw-handed, serpent-haired harlot whose look would turn one to stone. Following the battle, Pegasus leaped full-grown from the blood-soaked ground. Pegasus represents power, speed, and imagination, and his symbol has appeared on countless art works since ancient times.

In modern times, the Vacuum Oil Company in South Africa started using the name Pegasus and a line drawing of a flying horse in 1911 to represent the power, speed, and imagination of the horseless carriage. When Vacuum and Standard Oil of New York (both offshoots of the 1911 dissolution of John D. Rockefeller's mammoth Standard Oil Company) merged in 1931, they adopted Pegasus as their worldwide trademark.

The flying horse was used by affiliate companies as well, including Magnolia Oil in Texaco, headquartered in what was the tallest building west of the Mississippi in downtown Dallas. A sales manager of a Japanese affiliate suggested red as the color for the company's proud mount. No doubt he knew of the bloody origin of the mythological creature.

Many Texans and most Dallasites think that the Pegasus was placed atop the Magnolia Building to commemorate the Texas Centennial in 1936. Actually, the company ordered it as a flamboyant welcome to delegates to a National Petroleum Institute convention in 1934. Magnolia's advertising director called on their sign contractor, Texlite Company in Dallas, early in September 1934 with the order.

The meeting was scheduled for November 8, just six weeks away. As Texlite's treasurer and chief engineer, J.B. McMath had the task of designing, engineering, and erecting an unprecedented sign in record time.

Though lacking even a high school education, McMath followed in his father's footsteps as a sign maker. The elder McMath had painted the sort of signs that adorned brick walls and barns, indicative of advertising practices in the late 19th and early 20th centuries. J.B. was more suited, however, for the new generation of advertising signs. He developed uncanny empirical engineering skills which he used to design complicated porcelain and neon-lit signs.

A young woman artist at Texlite produced the 40-foot-long design of the Flying Red Horse, while McMath conceived the framing system, supports, and turning mechanism of the sign. He saw that if the image of Pegasus were produced with a single thickness of porcelain-coated metal sign, elaborate bracing against the wind 29 floors up would mar the clean lines of the soaring symbol. So McMath connected two signs, spaced eight feet apart, to cope with the high winds and to disguise the bracing between them.

This procedure gave rise to countless yarns generally proposing that there were two horses atop the Magnolia Building so Fort Worth wags couldn't say Dallas had become a one-horse town!

The two thin horses and their bracing were connected to a rotating mechanism that in turn was supported by a tower extending from the rooftop. The entire effect is simple and dramatic from a distance, yet delightful in detail when examined closer.

In earlier years, the Flying Red Horse could be seen from any approach to Dallas, by car, train, and by plane from as far away as Hillsboro, 60 miles south, according to pilots. Dallas' skyline was indeed unique with its own symbol for the city's power, speed, and imagination. But here came the Mercantile Bank Building, the Republic Bank, and others that aspired to greater heights than Pegasus. So the horse and its building slipped from the limelight. The oil company, changing all affiliate names to Mobil Oil in 1959, moved out of the building a few years ago.

But not before the city of Dallas recognized the historical significance of its old friend and protected it with landmark designation in 1973. Mobil gave the entire building to the city in 1978. It has since been sold to investors who are restoring the street façade and renovating the interior for first-class office space. The city has retained ownership of the sign. A familiar companion on Commerce Street was lost last year when the Baker Hotel was imploded to make way for a new Southwestern Bell Telephone building. The adjacent Adolphus Hotel, however, is undergoing renovation. Other new buildings and historical renovations are revitalizing the entire downtown area.

J.B. McMath and his wife live too far from downtown to see the sign from their front door, but they still keep tabs on their friend. He recalls the time his night lighting inspector phoned frantically with the news that the turning mechanism on the horse had broken loose and the neon sign had become a "whirling red blob."

Remembering how each section was hauled up on top of the elevators, carried out through the penthouse windows, and handed up to the roof, McMath says, "It frightens me today to look up at that sign and think of how we did it.

"But it is my greatest achievement, both in magnitude and in its ability to withstand the elements all these years."

Peeping through gaps between the taller buildings that surround it and bracing itself against the intrusion of those still planned to tower above his once exclusive heights, Dallas's Flying Red Horse is not only a symbol of the city's power, speed, and imagination, but of J.B. McMath's as well.

Chapter 15

The Final Chapter

Prelude: Grandaddy McMath died on December 17, 1982. I don't really remember much about it because I had just given birth to my third daughter, Robin the previous July and I was so busy with my three daughters that I hadn't been able to spend much time with Grandaddy. He had not been feeling well for several weeks and Charley had been to see him several times without me. Charley was going to graduate school four nights a week in addition to holding down a full time teaching job but he knew his grandaddy was declining and all the family tried to prepare themselves for it. We were all praying for his healing until one by one the Lord began to tell us that we should let him go because this was the time God was calling him home. As it says in Hebrews 9:27—"It is appointed for man once to die, and then his judgment." As soon as everyone in the family had let him go in their prayers, he died very quietly and went to heaven. I think you will agree with me that his was a life well spent.

I wanted to include this one article that was written by J.B. Sr. on February 1, 1975 out of sequence chronologically with the other articles because it fit here in the midst of his death and dying:

One day following a business meeting with an official of a large corporation, as I started to leave his office at the conclusion of our business, he remarked to me, "Mac, there is a question I have been wanting to ask you for some time." I replied, "Let's have it." And he asked, "Please tell me why you Christians are always shouting and praising the Lord, and are forever talking about all the wondrous beauties of heaven, as if you could hardly wait to get there, and at the same time run for the doctor every time you get a stomachache just like everyone else does, as though you were afraid to die?

I had known this man for a number of years, during which time we developed a fine friendship. He was a tireless worker, of unquestionable integrity, and strictly business as long as there was corporation business to transact, but when free, he could be somewhat of a humorist; he was fully aware of my religious background and Christian faith and always showed high respect for what I stood for. However, he asked me many biblical and religious questions from time to time, but in such a humorous manner that I could never tell when he was serious or sincere, but even so I always answered him as though I took him to be serious.

This was the last biblical question this man ever asked me, for he retired soon thereafter, and moved to Tennessee to live with a son, where he died in late December 1955.

I was convinced beyond doubt that he was absolutely sincere in asking this question, which I have termed, "Why do Christians Fear Death?" I base my conclusions on the fact that while I never before as much as thought of an answer to such a question, the answer nevertheless seemed to come to me as I gave it to him, and at the conclusion of my answer he very soberly replied, "Mac, I accept your answer to my question."

Therefore I believe God saw the sincerity of this man's heart, and wanted him to have the answer.

I believe that every Christian should be extremely careful never to take lightly a legitimate biblical or religious question asked by anyone regardless of how insincere they might appear; for you never know when the apparent insincere manner in which the question was asked, is not just a smoke screen in an attempt to conceal a hungry heart, who is seeking truth and answers to perplexing questions before making a public profession or commitment to Jesus Christ. Those who sincerely seek truth before conversion usually make good stable Christians, for they are more aware of what they are doing when they accept Jesus Christ.

In answering this man's question, I began by asking him, "Have you ever seen a single species of God's creation who has the breath of life that would not run, fight or do anything in its power to protect its self from death; yet no creature other than man, who is made in the image of God, has anything to fear or to look forward to after death. It is very remotely possible that any creature other than man hasn't enough reason to even realize that his eventual death is inevitable; yet God through his mercy, has for their protection apportioned to each of them sufficient instinct to resist with all their power anything that would jeopardize their existence. Now if all God's creatures other than man has nothing to fear after death, then what does he fear but death itself?

There are many scriptures to substantiate the truth of the fear of death, or the sting of death. There are many factors, which contribute to the fear in the heart of the Christian. However, no true born again Christian should have any fear of death, and if he does he should then very prayerfully search his heart before God, and repent of and make right anything he might find wrong, and after that if the fear continues he should ascribe it to the enemy, and rebuke him in the name of Jesus, and ask for deliverance from such fear.

Article from The Voice of Healing Magazine 1983:

John B. McMath, Sr., who designed and erected the historic Flying Red Horse atop the Mobil Building in downtown Dallas, died at his home Friday, December 17, 1982, from heart disease, according to the Dallas County medical examiner. He was 88.

McMath, co-owner of McAx Sign Company, was famous in Dallas business circles for constructing the Flying Red Horse sign—a symbol of petroleum excellence throughout the world—, which turned night and day. The familiar Dallas landmark since 1934 stood atop the 29-story Mobil building.

His funeral was held on December 20, 1982, in the Library/Prayer Chapel of CFNI dedicated exactly one month earlier. Sharing in the service were his pastor, Rev. Everitt Fjordbak, Dr. Freda Lindsay, and Reverend H.C. Noah. Burial was in the Restland Memorial Park.

Brother McMath was born September 12, 1894, in Magnolia, Arkansas and came to Dallas at an early age. He and his family later moved to Galveston and then to Marlin where he was a firefighter. He also worked in a blacksmith shop and ran a bicycle shop.

He came to Dallas in 1917 looking for a job and worked for the Dallas Fire Department for a few years before joining the Borich Company, a sign company that later was bought out by Texlite.

McMath was working for Texlite Company of Dallas when Mobil adopted Pegasus as its symbol and proposed placing a statue of the mythological steed on top of the building. J.B. McMath designed the translucent statue, which later became a historic city landmark known as the Flying Red Horse because it glows red when its internal lights are turned on.

His wife, Clara Mae McMath of Dallas, is still a faithful supporter and prayer partner of CFNI.

The Dallas Morning News, Service set for Neon Horse Designer McMath, Saturday, December 18, 1982

Funeral services for John B. McMath, a retired engineer who helped design and install the flying red horse atop the Mobil Building in Downtown Dallas, will be at 1 p.m. at Christ for the Nations Church.

Burial will be at Restland Memorial Park.

McMath died Thursday at his home after a month's illness. He was 88.

He engineered many major neon signs for companies throughout the United States. One of the best known is the neon Pegasus he helped design in 1934 while chief engineer for Texlite Sign Company. The red horse has since become known as a symbol of Dallas.

Born in Magnolia, County, Arkansas, McMath lived in several Texas towns before moving to Dallas in 1917. He never finished high school but learned much of his trade while working in blacksmith and sheet metal shops and as a sign painter and carpenter's apprentice.

After arriving in Dallas, he became construction foreman for the Borich Sign Co., then one of the few electric sign companies in the country. At this time, Borich was getting its signs from another company, but McMath convinced his company that he could make better signs for less money.

As a result, Texlite was formed in South Dallas in 1923 in a small building McMath built himself. McMath eventually became the company's treasurer and chief engineer.

In 1946, McMath and a man named Axilrod opened their own company, which eventually was called McAx Sign Co. In 1961, the plant was moved to McGregor near Waco, and one and a half years later he sold out and retired.

McMath drew up plans in 1934 for Dallas' red horse at the request of the Magnolia Oil Co. for a convention of the National Petroleum Institute being hosted in Dallas. The company wanted to make a good impression.

Five days before the convention, the horse was up except for the 1,161 feet of red neon tubing. A fire swept through the Texlite-plant, destroying all the tubing and plans.

An improvised neon tube construction operation quickly was set up, and McMath and his crew got up on the horse high above the downtown streets and cut and bolted into place a pattern made out of beaver- board. The sign was turned on in time, ready to greet conventioneers.

"It has stood a lot of storms," McMath had said proudly, "Yeah, there's been a lot of wind service on that old sign."

McMath was a member of the Rotary Club of Dallas and the Full Gospel Businessmen. He was a director at the Christ for the Nations Bible School.

He is survived by his wife, Clara Mae McMath of Dallas, a son, J.B. McMath, Jr. of McAllen; a daughter Rebecca Jane Allen of Dallas, two brothers, Pickney McMath of Houston and S.H. McMath of Madill, Oklahoma; a sister, Mrs. W.L. Snyder of Dallas, six grandchildren and 13 great grandchildren.

The Dallas Times Herald, Designer of "Flying Red Horse" atop Mobil Building dies at 88, Saturday 18, December 1982

John B. McMath, who designed and erected the historic "Flying Red Horse" atop the Mobil Building in downtown Dallas, died at his home Friday from heart disease, according to the Dallas County medical examiner. He was 88.

Services will be at 1 p.m. Monday at Christ for the Nations Chapel, with burial at Restland Memorial Park.

McMath was working for the Texlite Co. of Dallas when Mobil adopted Pegasus as its symbol and proposed placing a statue of the mythological steed on top of its building.

McMath designed the translucent statue, which later became a historic city landmark known as the "Flying Red Horse" because it glows when its interior lights are turned on.

In addition to the landmark, McMath designed and installed the movie marquees for the Esquire, Majestic, Wilshire and Lakewood theatres of Dallas.

McMath was born September 12, 1894, in Magnolia, Arkansas, and came to Dallas at an early age. His family later moved to Galveston and then to Marlin, where he was a firefighter, worked in a blacksmith shop and ran a bicycle shop.

He came to Dallas in 1919 looking for a job and worked for the Dallas Fire Department for a few years before joining the Borich Co., a sign company that later was bought out by Texlite.

Survivors include his wife, Clara Mae McMath of Dallas, a son, J.B. McMath Jr. of McAllen; a daughter, Rebecca Jane Allen of Dallas; a sister, Fanny Snyder of Dallas, two brothers, Pickney (Dale) McMath of Houston and Sam McMath of Madill, Oklahoma; six grandchildren, and 13 great-grandchildren.

Original Obituary from Dallas Morning News:

John B. McMath, Sr. Survived by wife, Mrs. Clara Mae McMath, Dallas; son, J.B. McMath, Jr., McAllen, Texas; daughter, Mrs. John L. Allen, Dallas; six grandchildren, 13 great-grandchildren, brothers Pickney McMath, Houston; S.H. McMath, Madill Oklahoma; sister Mrs. W.L. Snyder, Dallas, Services 1 p.m. Monday, Christ for the Nations Church, 504 Fawnridge, Rev. E.M. Fjordbak, Reverend H.C. Noah, Mrs. Gordon Lindsay, officiating. Burial Restland Memorial Park. Memorials can be made to Christ for the Nations, 504 Fawnridge, Dallas 75224.

Warner, Wayne, Pentecostal Evangel Magazine, John B. McMath Designed Mobil Oil's Historic Symbol, 28 April

Scanning the Dallas, Texas, skyline at night, one can spot a flaming red Pegasus—Mobil Oil's old symbol –flying between the skyscrapers. What is not generally known today is that a creative and devout Assemblies of God layman more than 60 years ago designed and erected the sign when others said it would never withstand Texas windstorms.

After engineers told sign builder John B. McMath in 1934 that the proposed 30 by 40 foot flying red horse atop the 29 story Magnolia Building was impractical and hazardous, McMath went to his knees for help. The answer came in a vision or dream in the night. McMath who traced his spiritual conversion to a Marlin, Texas, street meeting, later told the Dallas Morning News, "I give God the honor of helping me."

But McMath prayed for more than engineering help. Time was of the essence. He had agreed to design, build, and erect the unprecedented sign so it would be on top of the city's then tallest building for a petroleum convention in November 1934, only six weeks away.

Racing to beat the deadline, McMath and his crew on the morning of the convention carried the final pieces up an elevator and onto the roof where they tightened the last bolt and triumphantly turned on the power.

A few years ago McMath told a reporter that it frightened him to think back to 1934 when they were building the sign. "It is my greatest achievement," he told the reporter, "both in magnitude and in its ability to withstand the elements all these years."

Despite the skeptics, McMath's design, engineering skills, and faith in God have stood the test of time. Today his "greatest achievement" is a protected landmark, already outliving him by 14 years."

Afterthought: And this closes the story of an ordinary man who led an extraordinary life because of a supernatural God. This type of life is what we all can live if we strive to follow God and have a day-to-day relationship with his son, Jesus Christ. No matter what we choose to do trying to serve Jesus on a day-to-day basis will enhance our lives. I hope J.B.'s example of how he lived his life will be an influence on the rest of yours. We only have one short life to live so we should have our priorities set on things that have eternal significance. It follows that I should also include the ending of life for J.B.'s wife, Clara Mae. This article was written about her from a student, Virginia Smither, who knew her well:

Mrs. McMath was not on the staff at CFNI, but she was behind the staff all the way. Many know the faithfulness of she and her late husband in providing the financial encouragement to get CFNI started. Mrs. Lindsay, I'm sure, is grateful to her for her faithfulness in praying for CFNI. But I really wonder how many had the privilege of getting to know this gallant lady personally.

At an age when most ladies would say their part in life's spiritual battles were over, Mrs. McMath was still warring on with no thought of quitting. I had the special privilege of providing her transportation to the campus for a short time. What a privilege that was!

It was hard to carry on a conversation with this lady as she was always interrupting to say another prayer. She was one constant prayer all the time she was in my presence. The presence of the Holy Spirit was so powerful in her that I am sure my gasoline supply was multiplied many times over as we soared along on spiritual power instead of the natural. She prayed for me, members of my family, the Lindsay family, the staff members of the school (individually too, not just as a group), she prayed for different students who didn't even realize she knew they existed, she prayed for the speakers and for the meetings and for the different expansion projects.

She prayed for people she saw on the street. Once, when we saw a church under construction, she started praying for it, the pastor of it, and then proceeded to pray for each family in the homes we passed, claiming their souls for that church that they would all be saved. She would sometimes grab me by the hand and say, "Come on, honey. We need to pray for…" and off we'd go. Never once did I detect a smidgen of consciousness of the great service she was rendering in prayer. She simply saw a need and got on to it without procrastination. There was never any indication that she was being habitual in her prayers. She prayed with all the love of her beautiful heart.

Last year I had to return to the States on personal business. I paid her a visit to learn that she had lost her precious husband of such long standing. The beauty of the presence of her Lord radiated from her, rather than grief or self-pity. She could only hold up her Lord's goodness and share with me how He had blessed her in this situation. Then, after only a brief conversation relating to her, her face lit up and she, with great eagerness, began to question me at great length regarding the outcome of hundreds of different prayers for me and mine. I was overwhelmed that this great lady, who had not seen me in two years, could remember all the prayers she had said for me out of the thousands and thousands she had prayed. I was truly touched at this example of her sincerity and awareness.

Mrs. McMath, I want to thank you on behalf of all the staff and students at CFNI, both past and present, for your love, your prayers, your example, you commitment and complete sacrificial dedication that has played a far more important part than we are capable of realizing here on earth, in making CFNI possible for me, for the other students, and for the world.

And I thank you God, for the privilege of being exposed to this beautiful child of yours.

Virginia Smither

Since this biological sketch of Mae McMath was done so well by Virginia, I think this is a good place for me to include my story that I wrote about Grandmother Mae back in 2014 as her granddaughter who loved her dearly and appreciated her mentorship to me as a young woman. You will see the eccentric side of her as well as the spiritual but I think all of us have an eccentric side if the truth be told about us.

Grandmother Mae

Sometimes there are people who cross your path in life that make a lasting impression. One of the women in my life who mentored, loved and taught me much of what I have learned about being spiritual is my husband's Grandmother Mae (her grandchildren called her Grandmother McMath). When I think of her I think of the scripture from the beatitudes that says, "Blessed are the pure in heart, for they shall see God."

Grandmother Mae (full name Clara Mae Welch) was born to Marion Bee Welch and Alice Eugene Carter Welch on September 24, 1900 on a farm in De Leon, Texas. On her fifth birthday, after attending her mother's funeral, Mae was sent to live with relatives at 1814 Pearsall in Corpus Christi, Texas (two aunts). At thirteen Mae was sent back to Dallas to stay in a boarding house and make her own way in life. As providence would have it, she got involved with the Pentecostal outpouring of the Holy Spirit, and most of her time was spent at church or in church activities. She was engaged at sixteen to a man who was a Christian but who did not share her zeal for Pentecostalism. It was at this time in her life that she met her future husband, J.B. McMath at a Dallas County Jail ministry. He was a new convert to Pentecostalism, having been saved on a street corner in Marlin, Texas. When May first met J.B. it prompted her to put her engagement ring back in the pocket of her former sweetheart and soon thereafter she married J.B. When J.B. proposed to her he said to her, "Mae, could you ever love me enough to marry me?" She replied, "I passed "could" a long time ago!" They married on January 19, 1919 and always told people that they met in jail.

I heard stories about Grandmother Mae long before I met her. While I was dating my husband Charley he told me the story of how his grandmother took him to a funeral home with her when he was about ten years old to see someone who had died. She let Charley roam free throughout the funeral home and soon he found an empty coffin and began to ask grandmother what it was like being in one. She helped him crawl in and she shut the lid. He thought it was a great experience but I am sure his mother would not have approved!

When I finally met Grandmother Mae I was not disappointed. Though she was never what you would call a beautiful woman as she became older, she always wore an angelic smile and made you feel like you were the only person that mattered while you were with her. When anyone would visit her, she would run out to the back of her house before you left and pick you some of her lovely miniature pink sweetheart roses and wrap the stems in foil. This was an extra treat of her love that would linger with you after you left. One of her granddaughters, Heather, still has some of the petals from that rosebush in her mementos. Grandmother always held your hand and patted you and would introduce me as "her darling grandson's wife." I never saw her in anything but a dress. She had beautiful, thick hair and looked a lot like the Queen Mother of England. Sometimes her smile would be deceiving because she played the little old lady to the hilt. She would come over to visit and ask me to join her for a little outing somewhere. No one warned me not to get in the car with her. We would take off down the street and stop frequently whenever she saw some poor unsuspecting neighbor in their yard. She would tell me that they were my cousin and we were stopping to say hello, and I believed her. When we got out of the car she would talk long enough to find out her neighbor's needs and then she would have us all pray. It was a long time before I realized that I was not related to any of these people.

She was also a terrible driver. I would have to not look to the left or the right when I got in the car with her because she was a menace to all moving things around her. Actually, you didn't have to even get in the car with her for her to take you on a surprise visit. Grandmother lived in the prominent neighborhood of Lakewood in Dallas and she took me down an alleyway on her street one day and into a strange little back apartment that was a hint to come of the lady inside. The lady was very old, wrinkled, with lots of makeup and black hair dye. She was dressed in a black negligee set out of the 1940's. The room had a large bar and the walls were zebra-striped red and black. The lady had obviously been drinking from that bar most of the day. Grandmother Mae was oblivious to all around her and began to chat with the lady. Then she grabbed my hand and put it over the lady's and said, "Now, my darling granddaughter is going to pray for you." I didn't know much about praying at that time but I did what she said and prayed. Grandmother Mae taught me that all people have spiritual needs and to pray for them when they express a need.

Grandmother Mae never wasted a day in her life. She had a box in her living room full of wigs and instead of worrying about her hair she would just pop on a wig when she was ready to go somewhere. One morning she wanted me to take her to the neighborhood grocery store. I said sure and as she proceeded to get ready I noticed her hair was in terrible disarray. She climbed in the car with me without her wig and I was too embarrassed to say anything about it. When we got to the store she saw herself in a mirror and just had a good laugh about it. To say that she could be eccentric was an understatement.

She would take trips at the drop of a hat. My husband Charley remembered a time when he was a child when she took him to Memphis, Tennessee in her new black Cadillac (she didn't own a Cadillac of her own but granddaddy had a few over the years that were company cars) and this one had air-conditioning. The only trouble was that she would not turn it on. Charley said that she rolled the windows down for the whole trip to Memphis. The lesson she taught him was that when you went by a body of water the temperature would drop a little. He never forgot this science lesson from his Grandmother that he learned from experience.

When Charley and I were in college at East Texas State University in Commerce, Texas grandmother would often drop in on our hippie pad and bring us her newest religious material (she never threw any religious material away, she felt she had to give it to someone) and she brought enough for all our friends. I remember a time she came and we weren't home from classes yet, but there were some kids at our house and she began to chat with them, then they all held hands and prayed. Of course, these hippie friends said, "Wow, your grandmother is the most religious lady we have ever met!" It was on that visit that she gave me her china and crystal that she was gifted with on her fiftieth wedding anniversary. Things didn't mean much to her. I still have that Havilland china and it is one of the most precious things I own. Grandmother Mae gave another precious gift to her granddaughter Heather Davidson Danamaraj. When Heather was in college she came to visit Mae one day and Grandmother slipped off her wedding band and gave it to her. Heather wears it now as her own wedding band. It is a simple gold band with an etched pattern almost rubbed off from wear. It has an inscription which reads, "B to Mae 1/19/1919. It is the most precious item Heather owns.

Another time grandmother got on a Greyhound bus to go to California to visit a grandson in the military service just so she could go to church with him because he told her he had begun to go to church. It took her three days to get there. She spent the day with her grandson and went to church with him, then spent three more days getting home. She had left granddaddy a note saying she had decided to go to California. I'm sure that her grandson John Allen never forgot that trip. Later I found out there was a little more to the trip than just going to church. John tells that he was in love at twenty-two with a young lady named Connie who had a daughter named Cathy and that grandmother did not approve of the match. She must have prayed all the way back to California on that bus, because soon after that they broke up.

There were many examples of Grandmother Mae being liberated well before the women's liberation era. Though she had a beautiful home with beautiful furnishings she was never a cook or a housekeeper. Charley and I would quite frequently bring friends from college to her house to visit and go to church and we would never know what we would find. I remember one time when she asked us to eat with she and granddaddy and then began to look around for something to serve us. She had made a crock of potato salad that would have fed the multitudes of China and then she began to look for the sausage to go along with it. She looked in all the cupboards and drawers and had our friends in stitches laughing. When she finally found the sausage way back in the refrigerator we didn't know if we would live through eating it. Another time we were looking around in her refrigerator to find something edible when we spied a ham. It looked great but when we touched it, it disintegrated because it was so old! Her idea of cooking a meal was to go to Wyatt's cafeteria, which we did almost every Sunday. We lived about sixty miles away from grandmother and granddaddy in Commerce, and being starving hippies, we would all pile into cars and go to Lakewood Assembly of God Church on Sundays. Grandmother and Granddaddy would take the whole bunch of us out to lunch. Before we ate the meal we would have to hold hands and pray and then sing grandmother's favorite song, "This is the day." You haven't lived until you have sung that song and danced the Pentecostal shuffle in a very public restaurant. Grandmother Mae taught me not to be ashamed of my faith. She taught me that it never hurts to include a free meal in the deal to get someone to go to church, a tactic I still use to get all of my family to church!

Grandmother Mae's favorite thing to do besides going to church was to go to every religious meeting within a sixty-mile radius of Dallas. As grandmother got older and didn't drive anymore, she would take the city bus to her religious meetings. It was at one of these meetings that I learned another indirect lesson from Grandmother Mae. I had gone to a Women's Aglow meeting in Denton, Texas (My family was living there at the time) and found myself sitting at a table alone for a few minutes. As I sat there my mind began to wander to an issue that was bothering me at the time. I had some good friends that had inherited a lot of money and material things from a death in their family. Since at this time my family did not have very much money, I was very covetous and jealous of this friend. At about this time a lady approached me and looked at my name tag and said, "Gwen McMath, are you any relation to Mae McMath?" I said, "Yes, she is my grandmother." The lady squealed with delight and promptly called all her friends over to meet me. The Lord spoke to my heart at that moment and asked me which was better to have, a monetary inheritance or a spiritual one? I picked the spiritual and have never regretted it. I want to interject here that many years later when my mother-in-law died, I received many valuable things from her estate that had belonged to the grandparents. God double blessed me with both the spiritual and monetary inheritance at that time in my life. I learned from that experience that you can never out give God if you align your priorities with him, a lesson to learn even after both grandparents had been gone for a long time. Many times I would go to a meeting and there grandmother would be. I usually took her home, but if she could find someone going in the direction of another meeting, she would go with them. She knew every preacher and evangelist around, and the worst thing I ever heard her say about any of them was, "Well, they are controversial." Blessed are the pure in heart, for they shall see God.

There was no one who loved her children, grandchildren, or great-grandchildren more than Grandmother Mae. I didn't know for many years that grandmother had lost a child in an accident. This happened in front of grandmother's house when they lived at 2627 Pine Street. I only heard her speak of it once. She and I were outside sitting on a concrete bench when I told her it must have been hard for her to lose a child. She told me it was the hardest thing that ever happened to her. She didn't say anything more, didn't draw attention to her grief at all. Little did I know that I would lose a daughter and that one sentence she said then conveyed volumes to me about losing a child. I took my feelings of loss and bewilderment to the Lord and used my life to continue to serve the Lord. That advice of not becoming a victim made both of us strong women. When I had children of my own, we would go into Dallas from Denton and pick Grandmother up and she would stay with us for a few days at a time. I was always amazed that even though she was in her eighties she insisted on sleeping in the rooms with my children, and went to bed with them every night. I knew then that I wanted to be a grandmother just like her. My children are grown now and still remember with much fondness when their great grandmother would sleep with them. She was a grandmother who didn't mind her grandchildren playing with her things. All of the girl grandchildren remember playing with her hats, costume jewelry, and old mink stoles and muffs. Grandmother Mae gave me all of her old costume jewelry and I'm sure she exchanged it for a beautiful crown in heaven. One of her grandchildren, David Allen, who suffered from emotional problems as a young boy, would go and sleep on the floor next to her bed when he was troubled and she would pray for him. When she came to visit us, she would always have cash in her purse. She would cash her social security checks and then give the money away until there was none left. If she had a lot of money when she came or if she had just a little, she would give it to my children. She always talked to them about tithing and missions and many times after hearing her; they would give the money back for her to put in a collection plate somewhere. She used her purse to fill it up with food. This was her way of cooking, she would take the food back to granddaddy (he wouldn't eat it) or she would survive on it herself until the next meeting with food. We would take her to church with us and if there were refreshments she would fill her purse with them for later. None of my church friends ever forgot her either. They still talk of her emptying her purse in the collection plate and then filling it up with food! She taught my family about tithing and supporting missionaries.

Grandmother Mae would witness to all she came in contact with about how Jesus loved them and wanted them to give their heart to him. Many times we would get embarrassed or tired of her always talking about Jesus in every situation with anyone who would listen. I learned a lesson about this too. One day while at her house the phone rang while we were eating lunch and it was a neighbor who had lived next to grandmother about thirty-five years before. The neighbor was in the hospital dying and remembered how grandmother had witnessed to her so many years ago. She wanted grandmother to visit her again and talk to her about Jesus. This time she responded and gave her life to Jesus. I learned from grandmother to always take the time to tell others how Jesus loves them, no matter how embarrassing it might seem at the time.

When grandmother got into her nineties she could no longer live alone, so Charley's parents came back from the mission field in Mexico to take care of her. After several more years, when she was ninety-eight and could no longer see, she had to go to the nursing home. During her stay there, I never heard her complain, she just kept talking about her Jesus. I'm sure he was waiting with open arms when she died saying, "Well, done thou good and faithful servant."

Her obituary follows:

McMath, Clara Mae was born on September 24, 1900 and went to be with her Lord on Thursday, October 28th, 1999. An early Assembly of God pioneer, Mae McMath, along with her husband, J.B. McMath, Sr., now deceased was an active participant and supporter for Christ for the Nations, a local "Pentecostal" Bible College. She was also a charter member of the Lakewood Assembly of God Church. Mrs. McMath was noted in her church community for her kindness, generosity and ecumenical spirit. Ms. McMath is survived by grandsons John R. Allen, Jr.; Edward G. Allen, Carey Allen; John B. McMath, III; Charles C. McMath; a granddaughter Gwendolyn R. Davidson, and their spouses; 2 great, great, grandchildren; a son-in-law John L. Allen and his wife Rosemary; and a daughter-in-law Mildred C. McMath. Her husband John Bunyan McMath, Sr.; her sons J.B. McMath, Jr. and Edward McMath, daughter Rebecca J. Allen and grandson David Allen preceded her in death. Services are scheduled for 2:00 p.m. Friday, October 29, 1999, at the Sparkman Crane Funeral Home, 10501 Garland Rd, Dallas; Internment at Restland Cemetery, Greenville Avenue, Dallas.

Afterthought: I would like to tell you of the last time I saw Grandmother Mae. During the last year of Grandmother's life she began to decline in health. She became totally blind and it became hard for J.B. Jr. and Mildred to care for her. When she got to the point that she wasn't eating anymore the decision was made to put her in a nursing home. Of course, at this time the family all knew we probably wouldn't have her with us for very much longer, so we all began to come and go in the nursing home to say our goodbyes. My husband, children, and myself arrived at the nursing home one morning and told her we were there and she felt and loved on us. She, of course, wanted to pray, and we prayed for her. Then she wanted to sing, and with a beautiful clear voice she began to sing,

Count your blessings, name them one by one,

Count your blessings, see what God has done,

Count your blessings, name them one by one

Count your many blessings, see what God has done.

Her singing made me weep, here she was in a nursing home, blind and singing "Count your Blessings," from her heart of hearts. I pray that when I leave this earth, I will leave it with such humbleness as she did, praying and singing to a God who had always been there for her, even in her darkest hour.

Psalm 116:15—"Precious in the sight of the Lord is the death of his saints."

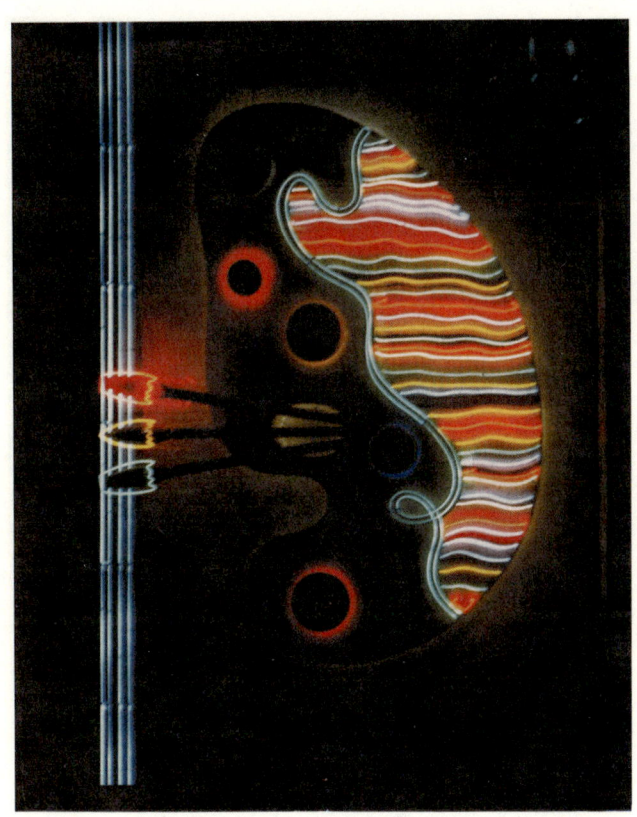

Esquire Theatre, Dallas.

FOREST THEATER
Established 1956 - Dallas, Texas

Chapter 16

Pegasus Finds a New Resting Place in Dallas

The original Pegasus that once perched atop the downtown Dallas headquarters of the Magnolia Petroleum Company from 1934 to 1999 now has a new home. The famous icon of the City of Dallas skyline now dazzles new visitors from its new location in front of the Omni Hotel, 555 South Lamar, Dallas, 75202. Restoration of the original panels began in 2013 and, now are complete with a new set of neon lights, it is now again a restored historical icon.

The office of the Cultural Affairs Interim Director David Fisher stated he was glad for the opportunity to display this cultural artifact once again.

This particular Pegasus has a storied history that dates back over sixty years and will now be placed at its namesake Pegasus Lawn for the entire world to see. While visiting the new area, visitors will see a large "B" and "G" in front of the Pegasus. Individual visitors are supposed to stand between the letters to be the "I" to complete the word "big". The Pegasus had remained on the roof of the Magnolia Building until the late 1990s. By that time it was in rough shape with broken neon tubing, rusted and damaged panels, and a platform that no longer rotated. In 1999, a crane and a helicopter aided in the removal of the two original 40-foot horses from the top of the Magnolia Building.

The City of Dallas mayor Ron Kirk and then senator Kay Bailey Hutchinson were among the private contributors who rallied around what was referred to as the "Pegasus Project." The idea was to complete the project in time for the new millennium. On January 1, 2000, the replica was officially lit, bringing the Pegasus back to life. There were over 200.000 people in the streets of downtown that night to watch the historic event. The original Pegasus was used as a template to create brand new winged horses for the city's 2000 Millennium Celebration, lighting the sky once again high above the Magnolia. However, when they finished using it as a template, no one seemed to know what happened to the original.

Omni Dallas Hotel developer Matthew Southwest went in search of the lost horses and finally discovered them in a city-owned shed near White Rock Lake.

For months, a team made up of the City of Dallas, Matthews Southwest and Tony Collins Art, worked the restoration and design of the new rotating Pegasus, which places the original horses atop a 22- foot oil derrick.

As a tribute to the memory of Matthews Southwest's vice president, Jeff West, and at a cost of $200,000, the fully restored Pegasus now rests in front of the city-owned Omni Dallas Hotel. To add to the hotel's interest, the Omni also showcases over 7,000 pieces of original, iconic Dallas art by 150 local artists throughout the guest rooms, culinary venues, and the hotel's common areas.

Afterthought: Should J.B. McMath look down from heaven today I think he would be delighted that the famous Pegasus is still glowing across downtown Dallas. Of course, he would be looking at the top of the Magnolia Building for his horses, but as his eyes settled and he looked around on the Pegasus by the Omni Hotel, he would be delighted to see the new horses made from the original ones and to know that no one had forgotten one of the most remembered icons from Dallas and the great state of Texas. For a man that wanted to leave his mark on the world, I think he would be proud of the secular Pegasus neon signs he was so famous for creating. But, on the other hand, he could look on over from Downtown Dallas to Oak Cliff and see the rotating globe that is the symbol of Christ for the Nations Institute and he would say, "That's the best one thousand dollars I ever spent." He would think he got a bargain for all the ongoing souls that are being saved as a result of that investment. As a proud Texan and a devoted Christian, I think he would thank the Lord for his guidance in his life to help build the Flying Red Horse because it led to so many people listening to his testimony about Jesus Christ as well as creating a genuine Texas icon for future Texan generations.

Charley McMath, grandson of J.B. in front of Flying Red Horse while temporarily kept at Farmers Market Dallas, TX

Dallas News staff photo by David Woo.

The commuter skyline

This sight is probably better known to Fort Worth and the Mid-Cities commuters than Dallas residents. It is the Downtown Dallas skyline at 7 a.m. taken from the Dallas-Fort Worth Turnpike. As the sun begins its daily climb, thousands of commuters flood into downtown with the sun in their eyes.

Credit: Michael Cagle

Outside Omni Hotel, Dallas Texas

NEON DREAMS

Prelude: This letter exemplifies J.B. and Mae's life as a whole—may we all be so blessed to be remembered in eternity in this way. May we all be the people God intended us to be, that's the key to true happiness.

5-9-96

Dear Mrs. McMath,

A very nice article about J.B. McMath appeared in a recent issue of the Pentecostal Evangel. At first glance my thoughts went back to the old church at Peak and Garland Streets where you were my Sunday school teachers. I couldn't have been more than 5 or 6 years old at the time. There were times when you and John would take me to your house on Pine Street for lunch but I think I was too bashful to eat.

The gifts are still in my memory. I remember a nice little handkerchief with pictures of nursery rhyme characters printed on it. One Christmas you gave me a green toy truck with battery operated headlights. The Sunday school picture cards were always nice. One day when John was taking me home from your house he dropped me off at the corner of Carpenter Street and Second Avenue. Before I got out of the car, John handed me a crisp dollar bill and said, "This might help buy some groceries." In those days a dollar would buy a lot of groceries. Such memories I will always cherish.

As for the article about John, I made a copy of it and put it above my desk for people to see. When glancing at it yesterday, I think the Holy Spirit spoke one simple word to my heart. The word is "integrity." If someone were to ask me to define the word, I think I would say, "integrity is J.B. and Clara McMath." That's the way I remember the both of you. The example you both gave to me is a gift that keeps on giving. It certainly has challenged me to take a closer look at my own life and try to be a better example than in some of the past. Integrity is adherence to God's absolute truth and principles and this is what I see and remember about the two of you.

My wife Billye and I think about you from time to time. She always mentions the beautiful smile God has put on your face for all these years.

We both want to wish you well. Thank you for just being the person God meant for you to be, and, for wonderful memories.

Love in Jesus' name,

Ernest and Billye Godwin

Author's Note

As I was researching for this book about my late husband's grandfather, the one thing that always eventually came up in conversations was other people's stories about The Flying Red Horse. It seemed everyone who lived during the era of The Flying Red Horse had a story to tell about the Texas Pegasus. So, if you have a special memory about the red neon horse, please e-mail me and let me know your story. I would like to compile them for another book or article. If you have a story you wouldn't mind sharing with me please e-mail me at gtmcmath@hotmail.com.